SAYING AND SILENCE

SAYING AND SILENCE
Listening to Composition with Bakhtin

FRANK FARMER

UTAH STATE
UNIVERSITY PRESS
Logan, Utah

Utah State University Press
Logan, Utah 84322-7800

Cover design by Barbara Yale-Read

An earlier version of chapter one originally appeared in *Symploké* 2 (winter 1994) and was reprinted in *PC Wars: Politics and Theory in the Academy,* edited by Jeffrey Williams (Routledge, 1995). Chapter three is a reworking of an essay that originally appeared in *Rhetoric Review* 13 (spring 1995). Chapter six, with a few minor changes since, originally appeared in *College Composition and Communication* 49 (May 1998), © 1998 by the National Council of Teachers of English. Reprinted with permission.

05   04   03   02   01   5   4   3   2   1

Library of Congress Cataloging-in-Publication Data
Farmer, Frank, 1951–
    Saying and silence : listening to composition with Bakhtin / Frank Farmer.
        p. cm.
Includes bibliographical references and index.
    ISBN 0-87421-414-9
1. English language—Rhetoric—Study and teaching. 2. Bakhtin, M. M.
(Mikhail Mikhailovich), 1895-1975—Views on rhetoric. 3. Report
writing—Study and teaching (Higher) I. Title.
PE1404 .F357 2001
808'.042'0711—dc21

                            00-012852

For my parents,
Maggie and Roscoe Farmer

CONTENTS

ACKNOWLEDGMENTS

The chapters in this book were written over the span of several years and thus represent a chronicle of a sometimes orthodox, sometimes idiosyncratic engagement with the ideas of Mikhail Bakhtin. They also represent, I think, a measure of how my particular struggles with Bakhtin are both reflected in, and refracted through, the momentous shifts in our disciplinary conversation over the last decade or so. On a more personal level, these chapters may even serve to chart those occasions when I have seen fit to change my mind about some aspect or consequence of Bakhtin's thought.

Yet more than this, the chapters gathered here represent a record of the people and universities who provided me with encouragement and support. I would first like to thank the English Departments of East Carolina University and the University of Kansas, both of which extended to me the kinds of institutional assistance without which this book would not have been possible. Nor can I begin to do justice here to the editorial advice and encouragement I received from Michael Spooner, whose optimism and patience sustained this project (and its author) through those predictable, but still critical, hurdles in its coming to print. I also wish to thank my anonymous reviewers for their thoughtful suggestions, as well as Red O'Laughlin for his valuable (and remarkably cheerful) help with all the last-minute preparations of this manuscript.

Over the last several years, there have been many colleagues who generously contributed to the completion of this manuscript—whether they did so through conversations about ideas, or through comments on earlier drafts, or simply through their abiding friendship and enthusiasm.

I would thus be remiss if I did not take this opportunity to thank Todd Goodson, David Stacey, Carol Mattingly, Bruce McComiskey, Sandy Young, Collett Dilworth, Pat Bizzaro, and Nancy Zeller. I especially wish to extend my thanks to Jeffrey Williams and Lillian Robinson for some of the most politically and theoretically challenging breakfast conversations I have known and to my former graduate students—Denise Machala-Woods, Tony Atkins, Deanya Lattimore, and Faydra Womble—for their collective ability to make me question my own certainties, even when they did not realize they were doing so. My thanks also to Devlyn McCreight, for his willingness to participate in the experiment that eventually became chapter two of this book.

Among Bakhtinians, I owe a debt of gratitude to Jim Zappen, Michael Bernard-Donals, and Andreas Kriefall. Caryl Emerson continues to amaze me with her professional generosity, and I cannot say enough about the many good turns—professional, scholarly, and otherwise—extended to me by Don Bialostosky. I am a better scholar for having had the opportunity to know, and occasionally work with, such exceptional colleagues.

And for Linda, intimate outsider, without whose loving perspective these words find no hearing, my deepest gratitude.

Note: Unless otherwise cited by keyword or full title, references to Bakhtin's texts use the following abbreviations:

AA = *Art and Answerability*
DI = *The Dialogic Imagination: Four Essays*
PDP = *Problems of Dostoevsky's Poetics*
RW = *Rabelais and His World*
SG = *Speech Genres & Other Late Essays*
TPA = *Toward a Philosophy of the Act*

INTRODUCTION

One development in recent scholarship centers upon what is often referred to as a rhetoric of silence. Not that we have just discovered such a rhetoric, for it is clear from even a cursory look at Richard Lanham's *Handlist of Rhetorical Terms* that our predecessors long ago established a whole family of words to describe the power that silence could effect in situations that were clearly rhetorical. Indeed, within this family of ancient terms, we find not only the obvious, *silence,* used in a rather specialized way, but also the far less familiar *obticentia, praecisio, reticentia, interpellatio*—all of which fall under the umbrella term, *aposiopesis,* a rhetorical figure that attempts to capture the persuasive effects of sudden silence. Classical rhetoricians apparently understood the strategic and dramatic purposes for which a refusal either to speak or to cease speaking might be appropriate, as evidenced in their constellation of terms for this one particular genre of silence.

But contemporary investigations of a rhetoric of silence have been largely (though by no means exclusively) tied to the project of recovering women's contributions to the history of rhetoric and rhetorical theory. This ought not to be especially surprising, given the status of women's discourse throughout much of Western history and women's long familiarity with silence as an ascribed quality of patriarchically-defined feminity. But of late, some feminist scholars have sought to reveal the communicative realities of silence, detailing, in particular, the ways silence has been creatively deployed by women rhetors and rhetoricians through the ages.

Cheryl Glenn's investigation of Anne Askew makes exactly this point. Tortured for her radical beliefs, the sixteenth-century Protestant reformist Askew developed a host of ways *not* to answer her brutal and cruel inquisitors. In *Rhetoric Retold,* Glenn argues that

Askew occupied a familiar position in a longstanding tradition of women's rhetorical silence, a lineage that continues today in such contemporary figures as former Texas governor Ann Richards and law professors Anita Hill and Lani Guinier, as well as former Surgeon General Jocelyn Elders—all of whom, Glenn points out, are quite accomplished in exercising silence as "a strategy of resistance" (177). Glenn wants to dispute the conventional reading of women's silence as always (and necessarily) the consequence of oppression, as strictly the muting of voices unheard. "Silence," Glenn insists, "is more than the negative of not being permitted to speak, of being afraid to speak; it can be a deliberative, positive choice" (176). Largely because "silencing and silence" are "rhetorical sites most often associated with women" (177), we have only begun to understand the historical and potential importance of silence as a rhetorical strategy.

As Glenn knows well, there is a profound difference between silence enforced and silence freely chosen. Yet, what's implied in her study (and others) is the possibility of a relationship that may obtain between these two modes of silence. Indeed, the history of women in rhetoric itself would suggest that *some* relationship must exist between enforced and chosen silences, for surely that special history is characterized again and again by this very tension. And, in fact, other feminist rhetorical studies do much to confirm this relationship. Julie Bokser's examination of Sor Juana Inés de la Cruz, the seventeenth-century Spanish nun and poet, for example, points the way to understanding something of the intricacies of that relationship.

In her reading of Sor Juana's autobiographical letter, *La Respuesta* (*The Answer*), Bokser details the context that prompted an exchange between Sor Juana and the bishop of Puebla, "Sor Filotea," a feminine pseudonym for Manuel Fernández de Santa Cruz y Sahagún. In the verbal guise of a fellow nun, Sor Filotea chastises Sor Juana for her "secular studies and her writing" (2) and urges her to desist from any further critiques of the church hierarchy. As Bokser notes, the bishop essentially tells her to silence herself. Sor Juana's epistolary reply, *La Respuesta,* is (not surprisingly) a text that is regarded as "her most explicitly feminist and polemical" (2). For in her letter, she takes up the issues of who may speak to whom, who may interrupt whom, who may choose not to respond to whom. By electing to answer the bishop, she has not only interrupted his discourse; she has interrupted the silence that he demands her to assume. In *La Respuesta* she tells the bishop that, not quite knowing how to respond, she has

> nearly resolved to leave the matter in silence; yet although silence explains much by the emphasis of leaving all unexplained, because it is a negative thing, one must name the silence, so that what it signifies may be understood. Failing that, silence will say nothing, for that is its proper function: to say nothing. . . . [O]f those things that cannot be spoken, it must be said that they cannot be spoken, so that it may be known that silence is kept not for lack of things to say, but because the many things there are to say cannot be contained in mere words. (41, 43)

In her gloss on these passages, Bokser observes that not only is Sor Juana making a general claim that all silences must be named if they are to have meaning, but Sor Juana is making this claim for herself, that is, for her own biographical silences. As Bokser points out, Sor Juana "interrupts the bishop in order to explain her past reticence and to announce her impending silence so that she herself will be listened to—by those who know how to hear" (5). And, indeed, Sor Juana writes very little after *La Respuesta,* a fact that does nothing to exempt her from charges of heresy leveled by an ecclesiastical tribunal two years later and for which transgressions she makes both public confession and a renewal of vows.

Like Sor Juana, the Russian language philosopher Mikhail Bakhtin understood all too well that the relationship between saying and silence is hardly one of uncomplicated opposition. Bakhtin realized that utterances were not confined to words, that gestures, sighs, yawns, exclamations, laughter—all such forms of wordless utterance were rich in their ability to answer and address others, to communicate meaning. Further, as if to emphasize this point, Bakhtin reminds us that "to a certain degree, one can speak by means of intonations alone." There are times, Bakhtin observes, when the uttered word itself has no semantic function whatsoever, except perhaps to serve as "a material bearer for some necessary intonation" (*SG* 166).

Though he did not pursue to any great degree the rhetorical possibilities of silence, he nonetheless understood that silences could speak, that silences could readily assume the position of utterances within what he refers to as the "chain of speech communion" (SG 84). Thus, the relationship between silence and the word, Bakhtin points out, is a qualitatively different relationship from that of the "mechanical and physiological" relationship occurring between quietude and sound. Because of their meaningful relationship, silence and word *together* constitute, for Bakhtin, a "special logosphere, a unified and continuous structure" of significance (SG 134). Bakhtin's further claim that "active responsive understanding" can simultaneously be a *"silent* responsive understanding" of action postponed only reinforces his viewpoint (however undeveloped) that certain silences can assume the function and status of the utterance (SG 68–69).

For Bakhtin, then, silence and words do not exist apart from one another, nor do the significances that we ascribe to each. That words can disturb silence in "personalistic and intelligible" ways, as Bakhtin claims must imply as well, that silence can disturb words in ways that are likewise meaningful (SG 133). Understood in this way, Sor Juana's *La Respuesta* is indisputably an eloquent, forceful rejoinder to the bishop's ecclesiastical cajoling. But it is her announced silence that may have proved in the end to be the more powerful utterance.

In what follows I offer a sampling of explorations into the relationship between the meaningful word and the meaningful pause, between the said and the unsaid, especially as this relationship emerges in our classrooms, our disciplinary conversations, our encounters with publics beyond the academy. Each of the chapters included here addresses some aspect of how it is that we and our students, colleagues, and critics have our say, speak our piece, often under conditions where silence is the institutionally sanctioned and preferred alternative. For my purposes, I have enlisted the potential of a number of Bakhtinian ideas to help in the project of interpreting the silences we hear, of naming the silences we do not hear, and of encouraging all silences to speak in ways that are freely chosen, not enforced.

Chapter one, then, examines the possible muting effects of certain widespread conclusions arrived at in the theoretical milieu of the past decade. Attempting to situate Bakhtin within the so-called theory wars that drove so much intellectual discussion in recent years, I draw extensively on one of Bakhtin's very early philosophical texts and later bring to the fore his concept of the superaddressee. I argue that Bakhtin offers us a third way out of the usual "closed loop" arguments that accompany debates about foundations by showing how theory itself is a function of the situated utterance, how every utterance is thoroughly steeped in normative evaluations, and therefore how dialogue is irretrievably joined to some conception of truth, however qualified that conception may be. Reviewing debates about foundationalism in composition (e.g., Bizzell, Smit, and most recently, Bernard-Donals), I try to show how the problem of *speaking truly* is never too far removed from what we ask of our students or what they ask of themselves—whether we realize this or not. In a time of regnant antifoundationalism, I argue, Bakhtin's commonsense observation that "every utterance makes a claim to justice, sincerity, beauty, and truthfulness" seems hopelessly passé, but this hardly means that our students are well served by dismissing such aspirations as nonsense (*SG* 123). For this reason, I conclude by showing that often, as writing teachers, we are the most readily available sounding boards for the many students who do embrace such ideals, and thus we often function in the role of superaddressees for our students. By the same token, however, we may discover ourselves to be the cause for students needing to find a superaddressee beyond ourselves and our classrooms.

The second chapter provides a concrete illustration of some of the issues raised in chapter one, especially those that address the silencing power of teacher authority. This chapter examines the difficulties faced by one student, Devlyn, who perceives his social and political views to be at odds with the views of his teacher (and a majority of his classmates). I begin by noting the tradition of "Aesopianism" among Russian artists and intellectuals, a manner of writing that has roots in the nineteenth century. As I explain, Aesopianism refers to a genre of camouflaged, oblique, deflective writing that seeks to say something, but only in an indirect, often coded manner (since doing otherwise could be extremely hazardous to a speaker or writer, especially during the Stalinist purges). Though I hardly mean to suggest any equivalence between the experience of my student writer and that of Russian thinkers writing under the most dire conditions, I do suggest an analogy. The problem for my student, Devlyn, was to find a way to express his views without tempting the institutional sanctions and penalties that may have befallen to him for doing so. Devlyn chose not to be silenced, but found ways to say what he needed to within circumstances that might not have been very congenial to his views. Drawing extensively upon one of his papers, I attempt to describe how he manages the rhetorical problem he faces and how his predicament complicates the too facile, naive, and supposedly unproblematic value of clarity in writing. The chapter ends with Devlyn's written response to my interpretation of his paper.

Chapter three begins by observing that there are alternative Bakhtinian frames within which we might understand Devlyn's struggles. Not only can we see them as illustrations of Aesopian strategies, but we can also understand them as evidence of Devlyn's process of transforming the "authoritative discourse" of Paulo Freire into his own "internally persuasive discourse." Along these lines, it becomes further possible to see Devlyn as [some]one who—already possessing a distinct voice—must [now] come to terms with the challenge that a new voice poses, a voice that is unfamiliar, difficult, and vexing, to say the least. To see Devlyn's struggles this way, however, demands that we come to understand voice in a specifically dialogic context. This chapter, therefore, explores a social, dialogic understanding of one of composition's venerable concerns—the problem of voice—by examining how Bakhtin and his contemporary, Lev Vygotsky, enable us to think about voice dialogically in three distinct but related aspects: developmental, rhetorical, and historical. After elaborating their respective ideas in each of these three senses, I conclude with a full discussion of how their ideas might be applied to the writing classroom, and, revising a caveat expressed long ago by Richard Lanham, I suggest that exhorting students to discover their one true voice may well result in nothing more than a confused and helpless silence.

Another of composition's long-standing practices is highlighted in chapter four. In the same way that Bakhtin's ideas enable us to understand voice differently, his conceptions of dialogue, I contend, enable us to reveal imitation as something more than "servile copying" or "mindless aping." Noting that several of Bakhtin's explicators in our discipline—Charles Schuster, Jon Klancher, Mary Minock, and others— have hinted at the possibility of revivified forms of imitation from a Bakhtinian perspective, I examine closely what Bakhtin said about imitation in his various works. I then attempt to show how dialogic approaches to imitation differ from our received understandings, outlining the distinguishing characteristics of what I call a dialogic imitation. What I suggest is that any dialogic understanding of imitation requires the student to take a position toward the modeled utterance, to be open to revising that position, and to come to understand the contingent, situational, rhetorical features of staking a position toward another's word, no matter how much that position might later be altered. To practice imitation otherwise is to practice the worst form of silencing.

Chapter five attempts to draw attention to how composition studies is constructed in public discourse and what we might say in response to how we are represented in popular media. Bakhtin's apparent belief that the gaze of the outsider is always kindly, beneficent, gift-bestowing, I argue, does not quite square with my experience that composition's outsiders seldom look upon our practices with a generous or neighborly point of view. After detailing three such perspectives, I note a second problem with Bakhtin's concept. In relying on the spatial metaphor of the "outside," Bakhtin has (perhaps unwittingly) formulated a potentially anti-dialogic concept, since dialogue, and hence meaning, require a temporal dimension as well. To make this latter point, I draw extensively on the work of C. S. Peirce as a way to restore the temporal to Bakhtin's idea of the outside. From there, I attempt to show why spatial metaphors, which govern so much of academic discourse, work against our ability to answer public criticism in any manner that could be regarded as truly dialogic. But, I conclude, our forays into the public sphere, if they are to be truly dialogic, must be not only responsive but also transformative, having the power to critically interrupt discussions about us and likewise the power to begin new lines of conversation. As I note, this will require a commitment to a better public sphere than the one we have now.

The final chapter explores the relationship between dialogue and critique as hinted at in the previous chapter. Arguing that dialogue needs critique as much as critique needs dialogue, I look at two key Bakhtinian concepts, anacrisis and the superaddressee, to show how these ideas accommodate elements of both dialogue and critique—the former, because it refers to the word that is capable of breaking silence and thereby of revealing the conventionality of the truths we embrace; the latter, because such a figure shows how the hopes we entertain of altered social conditions can be discovered within the most ordinary words we utter to one another. I elaborate the importance of both concepts in the context of student responses to a writing assignment involving a cultural studies approach to thematic materials. By closing with yet another examination of the critical and rhetorical significance of Bakhtin's superaddressee, I come full circle, returning to the focus of chapter one.

Here, then, is a sampling of attempts to identify how our many silences can be named and understood, whether those silences and their meanings happen to be about foundations or teacher authority; about whether voice *can* be taught and whether imitation *should* be; about public representations of writing teachers and writing students; about spatial metaphors and timely words; about cultural critique, its relationship to dialogue, and the relationship of both to social hope.

Indeed, if there is a single, guiding assumption that underlies these essays, it is that, within the dialogues we commence with our students, our publics, and ourselves, there is ample warrant for hope—hope that, through the words we share, the world we likewise share can be revised to include more voices, can be reimagined as a meeting place where, in Terry Eagleton's phrase, "people feel less helpless, fearful, and bereft of meaning" (184). It is my hope that these essays contribute to that end.

1 "NOT THEORY . . . BUT A SENSE OF THEORY"
The Superaddressee and the Contexts of Eden

[T]he only true reactionaries are those who feel at ease in the present.

Unamuno

LANGUISHING IN THE POSTFOUNDATIONAL

In the closing chapter to *Rhetoric in an Antifoundational World*, contributor and co-editor Michael Bernard-Donals observes that in our times, "the debate between foundationalism and antifoundationalism is moot; foundational notions of the human and natural sciences have been so discredited as to force us to consider what *kind* of antifoundationalism gives us the most productive and perhaps emancipatory knowledge" (437). In fact, as one reviewer pointed out, this collection seems to be largely devoted to the very project of identifying the sorts of antifoundationalism we are finally free to embrace, now that we have divested ourselves of foundational worldviews (Davis).

If Bernard-Donals is right, if the problem of foundations is indeed settled, passé, moot, then surely we must be very close to inhabiting the sort of antifoundational utopia imagined by Richard Rorty—a utopia where we no longer concern ourselves with truth and truth talk, where we no longer give legitimacy to the vocabularies of the philosophical tradition by contending with them (as rhetoric always has) in debate and dialogue. Surely, we must be very close to inhabiting that longed for moment when all of us consent to drop the subject of truth, and, following Bernard-Donals's suggestion, opt instead to direct our efforts to fine-tuning the sorts of antifoundationalisms that we may yet come to know.

That's one narrative explanation, of course, and a fairly compelling one, to be sure. But perhaps there are other narratives, other accounts that explain why disputes about foundationalism no longer seem to be in the forefront of disciplinary conversations. For example, what if our present reticence about foundationalism happens to ensue from the nagging realization that the question of foundations is not one that is so much decisively resolved as it is futile to pursue, a question that, at the end of the day, *cannot be arbitrated at all.* This realization ought to give pause to those who believe in the efficacy of both rhetoric and dialogue, especially if we are asked to concede that there is no apparent use for either in broaching the problem of foundations. Let me elaborate this point.

Because foundational and antifoundational worldviews constitute opposing and totalizing paradigms toward the question of truth, no mutually acceptable outcome could possibly be negotiated, and therefore no opportunity exists for the exercise of either rhetoric or dialogue. The contemporary philosopher Charles Taylor has perhaps made this point most emphatically by noting that in the disputes arising between advocates of truth-telling and truth-making discourses, "the interlocutors never reach a point where they (a) accept or find they cannot reject some things in common, which (b) sit with one worldview better than another" ("Rorty" 260). But to allow such a profoundly limiting condition of debate is to sanction the idea that these two worldviews are absolute, self-contained, incommensurable—each possessing, as Taylor observes, "the resources to redescribe everything which comes along, to reinterpret everything which might be thrown up by an opponent as contrary evidence, and hence to remain constitutionally immune to refutation" (260).

What Taylor describes is what I have elsewhere called a "rhetoric of subsumption," a rhetoric by which antifoundationalism is able "to insulate itself from any disputing contention, from refutation and challenge, from engagement and dialogue" (Farmer, "Thuggery" 220). Such a rhetoric, I maintain, holds enormous power over any disputing rhetoric that would call it into question and does so for this reason: when your worldview has within its own logic the resources to explain—or more exactly, to *explain away*—your interlocutor's worldview and when no adjudication of the question of foundations is even possible, then little remains but to drop the matter altogether, which is precisely what Rorty would have us do, and, indeed, what many of us have already done. Thus, understood this way, the promised land for rhetoric, its much awaited heyday when all foundations have been happily cast aside for good, when philosophy has at last become, in Rorty's words, "a kind of writing" (*Consequences* 90)—when all this comes to pass, our rhetorical utopia might seem to have been purchased at a very high price. For even while postfoundational culture promises to deliver the conditions needed for a full flowering of rhetoric, the disturbing fact remains that rhetoric seems to have had little, if anything, to do with the emergence of the very milieu in which it will supposedly flourish.

Notwithstanding its immunities, however, there have been those in rhetoric and composition who have sought to interrogate the conclusions of anti- or postfoundationalism. Bernard-Donals himself has called for an antifoundationalism that recognizes the material and extradiscursive, one that retains a place for rigorous scientific inquiry along lines proposed by Roy Bhaskar and his "transcendental realism." Some time ago, Patricia Bizzell warned that once foundational grounds for rhetorical authority have been critiqued and effectively dismissed, little of value remains in offering a "positive assertion of the good" (669), without risking the sorts of contradictions that could eventually result in "political quietism" (667). The problem, for Bizzell, finds at least a potential remedy in Linda Alcoff's "positionality" theory. Similarly, Reed Way Dasenbrock has expressed reservations about our casual abandonment of truth, especially when one of our central postfoundational orthodoxies—that all representation is misrepresentation—lands us in some rather thorny predicaments when we complain that reactionary critics of the academy misrepresent what we do. Even more recently, David Smit (after Donald Davidson) and Barbara Couture (after Edmund Husserl) have tried to salvage some usable version of a "truth" that we can live with.

I am not claiming that critics of anti- or postfoundationalism wish to return to a foundational golden age, nor do I subscribe to that wish myself. But I do think that a few observers of our present moment are very uneasy with the implications for rhetoric in a postfoundational milieu and have sought to find ways to cross the reportedly impassable borders between foundational and antifoundational discourses. In the following pages, I would like to return to the debates about "theory"—and by implication, foundations—that have occurred in the last fifteen years and try to recontextualize Bakhtin's concept of the utterance within those debates. Drawing upon a number of Bakhtin's ideas, but especially his "superaddressee," I will argue that a sense of theory is present in every utterance, that some notion of truth—however constrained, tenuous, or fragile—accompanies every act of saying; that is, I will try to revise one of our more prized commonplaces and argue that the uttered word is *normative* through and through, top to bottom, "all the way down," as the saying goes. I then conclude briefly with some thoughts on how Bakhtin's superaddressee illuminates this point and, moreover, illuminates the writing we receive from our students.

PARADISE (RE)VERSED

One of the recurrent metaphors found in the debates between theorists and antitheorists (a.k.a. New Pragmatists) is that of the biblical Fall, the moment when our mythical first ancestors disobeyed their Creator and promptly descended into sin, knowledge, and the burden of self-consciousness. On the last two of these misfortunes, it is not hard to see why such an image is eagerly appropriated for debates about theory. What may be surprising, though, are the realms assigned to each camp in these discussions.

I would offer, for example, that an outsider to these debates would most likely refer the theoretical camp to those otherworldly, paradisiacal realms commonly reserved for Laputans and other innocents who prefer to make their ideal home *elsewhere.* Correspondingly, pragmatists—new and old—would be assigned to the earthly realms of the fallen, the palpable, the mundane, where, happily for all concerned, the real work of the world gets done. Such, at least, would be a conventional, albeit broadly drawn, rendering of how the Edenic image might be deployed in present discussions.

What has occurred, though, is precisely the reverse. *Theoria,* it turns out, is our fallen state, while *Pragma* is the Eden we have fallen from (or, as it is more likely put, forgotten). The ironic fall *into* theory occurred when those first ancestors imagined the pristine wholeness of our original state to be divisible and, in fact, announced that only through such divisions can we know the world at all. The legacy of our Fall, then, is a kind of estrangement: the sundering of things whole and the misguided attempts at epistemology that such divisions require. In their provocative essay, "Against Theory," Steven Knapp and Walter Benn Michaels put the same point this way:

> The theoretical impulse . . . always involves the attempt to separate things that should not be separated: on the ontological side, meaning from intention, language from speech acts; on the epistemological side, knowledge from true belief. Our point has been that the separated terms are in fact inseparable. (29)

Much the same way that Adam and Eve willingly chose to escape the delights of the garden, Knapp and Michaels point out that "theory is nothing else but the attempt to escape practice" (30). The difference between the two is that, where our mythical progenitors were fabulously successful in their endeavor, champions of theory are doomed to a project of eternal failure. This is because, as Knapp and Michaels explain, theory "is the name for all the ways people have tried to stand outside practice in order to govern practice from without" (30). Since for Knapp and Michaels (and Stanley Fish, Richard Rorty, and others), no position "outside" of practice exists, the attempt is not merely futile but utterly self-deceiving. Once we dispense with our illusions, though, we are free to return to the paradise we never left in the first place, namely, practice. Here is the place where belief—or rather, true belief—is thoroughgoing, a place where, as Jonathan Crewe points out, "no knowledge can transcend or replace belief, which accordingly constitutes the highest epistemological plane on which the human mind can function (as God in his own way said to Adam)" (63).[1]

Here, I will attempt to reverse the reversal I have described above. Simply put, I hold that there are blessings to be had in restoring theory—or more precisely, *a sense of theory*—to its rightful locus at a necessary remove from immediate contexts. I will argue, then, that an Edenic otherness necessarily accompanies a sense of theory, and is, in fact, an inevitable function of the very conversation that presumably "stands in" for a thoroughly discredited foundationalism. To elaborate this claim, I will draw extensively on Mikhail Bakhtin's complex (and somewhat ambiguous) position on the question of theory and conclude by showing how his ordinarily mute superaddressee may have something to say about the debates regarding theory.

By now, few would be surprised that Bakhtin's ideas, in all their astonishing range, have been tailored to fit this debate. Nor should anyone be surprised that such appropriations are able to encompass the various sides of the debate. Bakhtin, to echo a common observation, has been successfully employed as a kind of belated spokesman for a dazzling array of theoretical projects and agendas. Predictably, he has also been recruited as a latter-day antitheorist, a pragmatist in the strong sense of one who denies foundational arguments for objective knowledge. To the extent, for example, that Stanley Fish casts Bakhtin as a thinker partially responsible for the "twentieth-century resurgence" of rhetoric and does so after claiming rhetoric as a strictly antifoundational concern (500),[2] then clearly Bakhtin (for Fish and many others) is allied to the pragmatist camp. Yet, while a good case can be made for Bakhtin the antitheorist, Bakhtin the theorist is never too far removed from his pragmatic double—an ambivalence succinctly captured in Bakhtin's own phrase: "not theory . . . but a sense of theory" (PDP 293).

BAKHTIN AS ANTITHEORIST

Bakhtin's very early meditation on ethics, *Toward a Philosophy of the Act* (1919-1921), is an appropriate place to begin establishing his pragmatist credentials. In this essay, Bakhtin refutes Kantian approaches to universal or categorical ethics, a position that he calls "theoretism." In contrast to the theoretical world, with its inevitable embrace of all that is generalizable and recurrent, Bakhtin speaks for the experiential domain of the act, the world he refers to as "once-occurrent Being as event" (TPA 10). For Bakhtin, authentic ethics resides not in principles, rules, or dogmas abstracted from experience, but in the answerable, unrepeatable *eventness* of lived life. And it is precisely this realm to which the theoretical is necessarily indifferent. As Bakhtin explains, insofar as personal existence is concerned, the theoretical world is not habitable:

> In that world I am unnecessary; I am essentially and fundamentally non-existent in it. The theoretical world is obtained through an essential and fundamental abstraction from the fact of my unique being and from the moral sense of that fact—"as if I did not exist" . . . it cannot determine my life as an answerable performing of deeds, it cannot provide any criteria for the life of practice, the life of the deed, for it is *not* the Being *in which I live,* and if it were the only Being, *I* would not exist. (9)

Another way to put this is that the theoretical is wholly alien to that which is particular and unrepeatable in my life as I live it; and, so being, the theoretical must account for my life in ways that are not just ethically untenable, but impossible. My life from a theoretical viewpoint must always be a generalizable entity, a finality. And *that,* Bakhtin points out, is not the life I live.

Bakhtin's animosity toward a theoretical ethics is unmistakable. But, as Bakhtin might add, there should be no great surprise in discovering that such an ethics exists, for the most important—and lamentable—inheritance of Enlightenment rationalism is its exclusion of what cannot be generalized. He thus notes that "it is an unfortunate misunderstanding . . . to think that truth . . . can only be the truth . . . that is composed of universal moments; that the truth of a situation is precisely that which is repeatable and constant in it" (*TPA* 37). *Toward a Philosophy of the Act* inaugurates Bakhtin's search for a version of truth that is neither universal nor repeatable, but rather one able to account for the particular and situational—the "once-occurrent event of Being" (61).

This search leads Bakhtin to formulate what he calls an "architectonics," a way to generalize the particular without compromising its very particularity, its concreteness. Bakhtin thus wants to establish a means to link together the "concrete event-relations" that characterize the nontheoretical world of particularized experience, while avoiding the systematicity and indifference to lived life that characterize the theoretical world. Gary Saul Morson and Caryl Emerson thus explain that "architectonics is not a matter of general concepts or laws," but instead a paradoxical attempt to find the "general aspects of particular acts" without surrendering their concrete quality as lived events (*Rethinking* 22). Bakhtin's project, according to Morson and Emerson, was how to answer the question, "What can we say in general about particular things except that they *are* particular?" (22).

Though his architectonics does not provide a satisfactory answer to that question, Bakhtin's early conceptualization of the problem leads him to think about it in terms of aesthetic as well as self-other relationships. These concerns about developing an architectonics persist and find more development in other essays of the period, especially "Author and Hero in Aesthetic Activity." But it is in *Problems of Dostoevsky's Poetics* that Bakhtin first reconsiders the possibility of another kind of truth through what will become the central theme of his mature work, *dialogue*.

From a Bakhtinian perspective, a dialogic truth is obliged to resist all those other versions of truth that, say, locate it *above* us (as in theological certitude), *outside* us (as in empirical "findings"), *inside* us (as in Romantic and psychological constructions of essential selfhood), or *behind* us (as in the received wisdom of authoritative discourses). What these various *topoi* of knowledge share, Bakhtin might point out, are answers that neither require nor invite a response. Each posits a finished version of what the truth is (or how it will be found), and thus each precludes genuine exchange. Finalized conceptions of truth render dialogue unnecessary.

Where, then, does Bakhtin locate truth, and what are the special features of a dialogic truth? Keeping with this spatial metaphor, Bakhtin situates truth in the territory *between* us, thereby making our understanding of truth both a function and a product of social relations. Of course, not all social conceptions of truth are necessarily dialogic, but all dialogic conceptions of truth are social. To put this in the most basic of terms, *one needs an other for truth to be*.

One of the first illustrations of a dialogic truth, Bakhtin observes, can be found in the early Socratic dialogues. In particular, this genre exemplifies "the dialogic nature of truth and the dialogic nature of thinking about truth. The dialogic means of seeking truth is counterpoised to *official* monologism, which pretends to *possess a ready-made truth*. . . . Truth is not born nor is to be found in the head of an individual person, it is born *between people* collectively searching for truth, in the process of their dialogic interaction" (*PDP* 110).

For those accustomed to regarding Platonic epistemology as perhaps the most extreme foundationalism, Bakhtin's lauding of Socrates will likely come as a surprise. Yet, Bakhtin emphasizes the point that while the "content [of individual dialogues] often assumed a monologic character," Socrates himself did not assume the role of one who had exclusive possession of a "ready-made truth." What accounts for this disparity is that the early dialogues had "not yet been transformed into a simple means for expounding ready-made ideas," but with the increasing monologization of later dialogues, the Socratic genre "entered the service of the established, dogmatic worldviews of various philosophical schools and religious doctrines" (*PDP* 110).

Again we sense Bakhtin's hostility to what he once called theoretism, but now refers to as "philosophical monologism," that abstract plane of reasoning that promotes truth as something capable of excluding human beings altogether. In this familiar scheme of things, truth has no need for multiplicities, for concrete variations, for individual consciousness. It follows that "in an environment of philosophical monologism . . . genuine dialogue is impossible as well." What Bakhtin wants instead—and what he finds in the work of Dostoevsky—is a truth "born at the point of contact among various consciousnesses," one that "requires a plurality of consciousnesses, one that cannot be fitted into the bounds of a single consciousness" (*PDP* 81). This is a truth not of objects, abstractions, or subjective empiricism, but a truth created and sustained through dialogue. This is a truth that resists all absolute and monologic formulations. This is a truth with people in it.

For pragmatists and other antitheorists, it is also a truth that refuses the original sin of theory, that is, the temptation to imagine itself able to stand outside practice, or for Bakhtin, outside dialogue. On this matter alone, Bakhtin clearly establishes his worth as a pragmatist of the first order. But more than that, Bakhtin's lifelong resistance to theoretism or philosophical monologism, his efforts to identify another kind of truth through dialogic relations, and his understanding of truth as a mutual enterprise, an unceasing process rather than a ready-made product would all seem to commend him thoroughly to an antitheoretical position.

What reason, then, to even consider the prospect of Bakhtin as an advocate of theory? Why is a sense of theory necessary to dialogue?

BAKHTIN AS (RECALCITRANT) THEORIST

Despite his polemics against abstraction, systematicity, and the theoretical, Bakhtin never dismisses theory as nonexistent or unimportant. Bakhtin acknowledges (implicitly or otherwise) that while theory runs counter to his own projects, theory nevertheless helps to define and clarify those projects. However, Bakhtin's characteristic move is *to acknowledge the reality of theory in order to subsume its claims to the more important exigencies of dialogue.*

This move is apparent early on. Recall that Bakhtin takes care to show how the realm of theory is incapable of explaining the concrete realm of particularity—the once-occurrent event of Being that constitutes lived life—and further, that "all attempts to surmount—from within theoretical cognition—the dualism of cognition [theoretism] and life . . . are utterly hopeless." Life cannot be lived in theoretical categories, and Bakhtin suggests that all our efforts to do so resemble "trying to pull oneself up by one's own hair" (*TPA* 7).

But does this mean that the theoretical plane should be dismissed altogether or that it can in no wise enter into the event of my life? Bakhtin answers no to both questions. As to the first, Bakhtin claims that theory's "autonomy is justified and inviolable" so long as it "remains within its own bounds." The problem arises, Bakhtin observes, when the theoretical "seeks to pass itself off as the whole world . . . as a first philosophy *(prima philosophia)*"—what we might be tempted to call a foundational truth (*TPA* 7-8). (Bakhtin seems not merely to acknowledge but to endorse a nonfoundational brand of theory—an option not always granted to combatants in the theory wars, who *demand* an allegiance to one side or the other.) As to the second question, while Bakhtin argues that "any kind of *practical* orientation of my life within the theoretical world is impossible," he does believe it possible for the theroretical to be interiorized as a "constituent moment" of life as event (*TPA* 9). Possible, yes, but not easily realized, and certainly not to be confused with pragmatism's attempts to do the same. Indeed, Bakhtin holds that "pragmatism in all its varieties" tries to turn one theory

> into a moment of another theory, and not into a moment of actual Being-as-event. A theory needs to be brought into communion *not* with theoretical constructions and conceived life, but with the actually occurring event of moral being—with practical reason, and this is answerably accomplished by everyone who . . . accepts answerability for every integral act of his cognition. (*TPA* 12)

Bakhtin makes clear that a pragmatist subsumption of theory is, in effect, nothing more than an instance of one theory attempting to contain (preempt? erase?) another—an argument that, not surprisingly, has found expression in the current debate, whether from the viewpoint of a pragmatist subsumption of theory (see, for example, Fish 315-41) or a theoretical subsumption of practice (see Rosmarin). Bakhtin, though, has little truck with either theoretism or pragmatism on this count, since both share a predilection to conceptualize life from without. Still, he argues, it is possible for theory to become a constituent moment in the event of Being, but not exactly in the way a pragmatist might wish.

To fit itself to practice, for example, theory must surrender its claims to an "outside" truth, since practice "denies the autonomy of truth and attempts to turn truth into something relative and conditioned" (*TPA* 9). Paradoxically, when that occurs, truth can no longer be incorporated into concrete existence, for as Bakhtin argues, "it is precisely on the condition that it is pure that truth can participate answerably in Being-as-event; life does not need a truth that is relative from within itself" (*TPA* 10). Thus, truth must keep some quality of absoluteness for it to be gathered into the event of a life, to make it something capable of being answered with my Being. Anything less will require me to hand over my experience to a relativism whose equivalence of potential truths is just as indifferent to my "living his-toricity" as a theoretism that offers external, moral guidelines.[3] When Bakhtin later rethinks this problem in terms of dialogue, he arrives at a similar conclusion: "that both relativism and dogmatism equally exclude all ... authentic dialogue, by making it either unnecessary (rel-ativism) or impossible (dogmatism)" (*PDP* 69).[4]

Make no mistake, there is a place for theory in Bakhtin, but not in the fashionable impulse to redefine it as just another kind of practice. That proviso effectively robs theory of the one quality that makes it theory—its claim to an outside knowledge, perspective, or truth. The place for theory, rather, is found when its very "outsidedness" is delivered into the event of living, when theory is subsumed not merely into practice, but into the unrepeatable event of lived life, into that quality ("surplus") of existence beyond the conceptions of either theoretism or pragmatism.

It would be convenient—and not entirely mistaken—to explain Bakhtin's critique of theory as the ruminations of a not yet fully-matured thinker. That, unfortunately, does little justice to the decid-edly mature task that Bakhtin poses for himself, namely, how to make theory human, how to make theory a constituent dimension of lived life, while avoiding the trappings of a relativism that trivializes being. The same problem, I believe, informs Bakhtin's search for a dialogic truth in *Problems of Dostoevsky's Poetics* and can be evidenced in other essays of the period as well. To dismiss these early arguments support-ing a theoretical quality to lived life as simply immature is to ignore the fact that Bakhtin frequently returns to old problems and themes to elaborate, develop, and recontextualize them and to maintain an ongoing dialogue with them.

The questions, then, are whether Bakhtin returns to the problem of theory as a legitimate intellectual activity, and if so, whether he regards it favorably. My response to both inquiries is a qualified yes, if first we grant Bakhtin his stated preference, "not theory ... but a sense of theory,"[5] and if second we identify where this sense of theory is subsumed not merely as a constituent moment of lived life, but of *life lived in dialogue.*

First, what does Bakhtin mean by a sense of theory? One clue may be gleaned by drawing an analogy with a related problem Bakhtin raises in the Dostoevsky book. Shortly after his comment on theory, Bakhtin follows with a parallel statement about Dostoevsky's understanding of faith: to wit, "not faith . . . but a sense of faith." Fortunately, *this* comment is more developed and thus more illuminating. The full excerpt reads: "Not faith (in the sense of a specific faith in orthodoxy, in progress, in man, in revolution, etc.), but *a sense of faith,* that is, an integral attitude (by means of the whole person) toward a higher and ultimate value" (294). Notice that "faith," in its first sense, is a content-laden abstraction, something ready-made and available for immediate use, notwithstanding its existence on a plane utterly removed from the one where life is lived. Notice, as well, that "a sense of faith" is something quite distinct, not a recycling of hand-me-down assurances, but an "attitude" toward "an ultimate value," and thus something fraught with difficulty (if only because the integration of this value requires that my "whole person" be prepared to answer its demands).

By analogy might we not suppose that Bakhtin's distinction between theory and a sense of theory follows suit from his parallel distinction between faith and a sense of faith? May we not reasonably say that theory, in its first sense, is all monologic truth that offers finalized knowledge from without, while a sense of theory is that "integral attitude" toward a truth that posits ultimate values to which our lives are, in some degree, answerable? If this is so, where then may Bakhtin's sense of theory be found, especially after dialogue becomes the overarching motif of his work?

AN "INVISIBLY PRESENT THIRD PARTY"

Among the many features of Bakhtin's conception of the utterance, the one that receives least attention is, no doubt, the superaddressee. In a late essay, Bakhtin introduces this concept by observing that within every utterance there is a presumed *third* listener, one beyond the addressee, or second listener, to whom the utterance is immediately addressed:

> But in addition to this addressee (the second party), the author of the utterance, with a greater or lesser awareness, always presupposes a higher

superaddressee (third), whose absolutely just responsive understanding is presumed, either in some metaphysical distance or in distant historical time (the loophole addressee). In various ages and with various understandings of the world, the superaddressee and his ideally true responsive understanding assume various ideological expressions (God, absolute truth, the court of dispassionate human conscience, the people, the court of history, science, and so forth). (*SG* 126)

Those few commentators who take the trouble to gloss these passages at all seem to recognize, along with Bakhtin, that the superaddressee negates the prospect that what I utter may be meaningless, which is to say, without meaning for *another*. Michael Holquist, for example, explains that "poets who feel misunderstood in their lifetimes, martyrs for lost political causes, quite ordinary people caught in lives of quiet desperation—all have been correct to hope that outside the tyranny of the present there is a possible addressee who will understand them" (38). Morson and Emerson likewise see the function of this third party as one of hope, or more exactly, the *necessity of hope* (*Prosaics* 135).

But why necessity? Bakhtin points out that the word, more than anything else, "always wants to be heard," and if that hearing is not to be found in immediate contexts, the word will press on "further and further (indefinitely)" until it locates a point of understanding. The profound importance of this observation is underscored when Bakhtin describes "the Fascist torture chamber or hell in Thomas Mann [as] an absolute *lack of being heard*, as the absolute absence of a *third party* [superaddressee]." One reason that Bakhtin passingly refers to the superaddressee as "the loophole addressee" is that the speaker (or author) can ill afford to "turn over his whole self and his speech work to the complete and *final* will of addressees who are on hand or nearby" (*SG* 126-27). The risk here for the speaker (or author) is not only that what he or she says will be misunderstood, but rather that what is said will be misunderstood *utterly* and *forever*. The superaddressee thus offers a loophole for a perfect understanding *elsewhere* and a hedge against the dangers of a consummated misunderstanding *here*.

Now, the temptation might be to regard the superaddressee—and the remote contexts in which he or she may be found—as a regrettable lapse into a naive idealism or transcendentalism, or perhaps even worse, an unapologetic solipsism. But to dismiss Bakhtin's formulation on these counts would be simplistic for a number of reasons. First, Bakhtin attempts, however briefly, to historicize the many forms the superaddressee may assume when invoked by a given speaker. Second, Bakhtin explicitly denies that the superaddressee *must* be a "mystical or metaphysical being," but allows that "given a certain understanding of the world, he can be expressed as such." Finally, Bakhtin's catalogue of possible superaddressees appears, on balance, to be indifferent to the entire issue of foundational truth. While "absolute truth," "God," "science," and "human conscience" all seem to fit easily into a foundational paradigm, other superaddressees, such as "the people" or the "court of history," may just as easily be interpreted as constructionist or antifoundational (*SG* 126). Indeed, the issue of foundational truth seems to have little to do with the actuality of the superaddressee (though it may have much to do with the form assumed by the superaddressee in any utterance).

For Bakhtin, what is important about the superaddressee is that "he is a constituent aspect of the whole utterance" and thus an inevitability of speaking or authoring (*SG* 126-27). What is important for my purposes, though, is that *the superaddressee is the incarnation of that sense of theory when it is subsumed into the utterance, into living, dialogic relations.* As such, the superaddressee reveals an "integral attitude (by means of the whole person) toward a higher and ultimate value" and thus constitutes that someone or someplace *else* to which I am answerable— answerable now in at least two important senses.

I am answerable in the sense that my construction of any utterance is determined by how I anticipate being received not only by my second listener, but also by my *third* listener—the superaddressee of my choosing, who, though not capable of an immediate response, is nonetheless manifested in my utterance by virtue of my need to posit an ultimate understanding beyond my present situation.[6] Bakhtin seems especially intrigued by that speaker who "fears the third party and seeks only temporary recognition . . . from immediate addressees," especially when one's immediates can at best offer only "responsive understanding of limited depth" (*SG* 127). In terms of the present argument, when subsumed into living dialogue as a sense of theory and incarnated in the utterance as the superaddressee, theory provides what it has always claimed to provide: *other* vistas, *other* horizons, *other* contexts for understanding beyond those that occupy "the tyranny of the present." Bakhtin seems to find especially odd (if not superficial) those who remain content to be heard within their immediate context alone, who feel no apparent need to appeal to an ultimate listener of any kind.

But another sense of answerability is at stake here, too—one that resurrects Bakhtin's early concern with responsible action. The positing of a superaddressee, of course, cannot help but to imply a certain ethical orientation toward the ultimate values embodied in the very superaddressee one chooses. Yet, the ethics born of the dialogic relationship with a superaddressee are *not* the ethics of theoretism, the ready-made principles, rules, edicts of a hand-me-down morality. Though any utterance may well subsume aspects of a theoretical ethics as a constituent moment of life in dialogue, whatever truth the superaddressee holds *for me* is as unrepeatable as every utterance I speak. And while Bakhtin hints that superaddressees are historically formed and are therefore susceptible to some degree of continuity, this does not change the fact that no particular superaddressee could possibly exist on the "theoretical plane." Moreover, because a superaddressee "embodies" my "integral attitude" toward a value (or values) that I regard as ultimate, the superaddressee always *requires* something from me.

A measure of commitment, then, inheres in the very concept of a superaddressee. To be sure, that measure may be quite innocuous, going no further than the tonalities that express a speaker's attitude toward what he or she regards most highly—keeping in mind, as Kenneth Burke pointed out some time ago, that our attitudes are always *incipient* acts (20). At the other end of the spectrum, though, and as Michael Holquist has shown, the superaddressee may make very dramatic, severe demands on our "whole person." Holquist, as I noted, refers to "martyrs for lost political causes," but it is not difficult to imagine other circumstances where, on behalf of a superaddressee who hears our pleas for justice or freedom or God or love, countless individuals throughout human history have answered with their lives. It would be foolish, of course, to posit the act of giving up one's life as a requirement for authentic commitment. But I am inclined to think that Bakhtin might point out that it is virtually impossible to conceive surrendering one's life on behalf of, say, the ontological proof for God or the categorical imperative (theoretism)—just as impossible, in fact, as trying to imagine giving up one's life for the judgments of an interpretive community or the conversation of mankind (pragmatism).

IRONIES OF EDEN

In *Philosophy and the Mirror of Nature*, Richard Rorty asks us to lay claim to a new Eden, one that exiles the philosopher as "cultural overseer who knows everyone's common ground . . . who knows what everyone else is really doing whether they know it or not, because he knows about the ultimate context (the Forms, the Mind, Language) in which they are doing it" (317-18). When this insurrection is accomplished, we will be free to return to what is the only ultimate context available: "If we see knowing not as having an essence to be described . . . but rather as a right, by current standards, to believe, then we are well on the way to seeing *conversation as the ultimate context* within which knowledge is to be understood" (my emphasis, 389).

Now, first, what does it mean to equate knowing with a right to believe? Are we not stumbling into the same tautological problems that Jonathan Crewe describes in reference to Knapp and Michaels, namely that "what is truly believed becomes equivalent to truth, while truth becomes equivalent to what is truly believed" (64n)? Crewe observes that in this pragmatist vision of the world, belief has a "kind of fullness and immediacy" that makes it wholly sufficient to all believers. Which is to say (and to say ironically, as Rorty would point out) that pragmatist believers are quite comfortable in their knowledge that what is believed is never anything more than a belief. In other words, they happily assent to the prospect that *in no other context* is it possible for their beliefs—say, in an unpublished poem, in a struggle against oppression, in that *too* controversial or unorthodox idea, etc.—to be in some way *true*. Crewe suggests that this is a rather idealistic formulation of belief, since belief has for us a decidedly "proleptic character." As Crewe puts it, "a *lack* . . . of justifying knowledge or 'groundedness' is implicit in the conception [of belief]" (64n).

I would argue that the lack alluded to by Crewe is the selfsame lack that Bakhtin mentions when he describes hell as an "absolute *lack of being heard*, as the absolute absence of *a third party.*" It is the very lack that the superaddressee is called upon to fill when we speak to others. It is the very lack that a pragmatist version of believing must ignore or deny, since a belief in contexts where a more perfect understanding is possible smacks too much of epistemological foundations. Crewe, interestingly enough, understands this lack in terms remarkably similar to Bakhtin's. Prolepsis, after all, is from the Greek rhetorical tradition and refers to the speakerly practice of "foreseeing and forestalling objections in certain ways" (Lanham 120). In couching this lack in terms of prolepsis, Crewe echoes Bakhtin's favored word, "answerability," thereby lending force to the notion that justification is always, to some extent, a function of a necessary third party in dialogue and in dialogic relations.[7]

But isn't Rorty's "conversation of mankind" an affirmation of dialogue as well? To be sure, Bakhtin is especially close to Rorty when searching for a dialogic truth to oppose philosophical monologism. Here and elsewhere, there are points of intersection that are indeed noteworthy.[8] But, as I have tried to show, one important difference between the two is that, whereas for Rorty "*conversation* [is] the ultimate context," for Bakhtin, an ultimate context may be found within every utterance, insofar as that utterance invokes a superaddressee, who understands perfectly what one has to say.

Every conversation (or dialogue), Bakhtin might say, is teeming with ultimate contexts; there is no separating the normative from the spoken. Or, as the contemporary philosopher, Hilary Putnam, has pointed out: "We always speak the language of a time and place; but the rightness and wrongness of what we say is not *just* for a time and place" (247). If this were not the case, we would face the curious necessity of having to attach a subtextual rider to every utterance we make, a disclaimer of sorts that might be translated thus: "Of course, you must realize that the words I speak to you have no meaning beyond the here and now in which they are spoken. That is, my words are thoroughly and irrevocably contingent on the context we occupy together, and to imagine that they have meaning in any future context is to tempt the illusion that my words transcend situation, circumstance, and history."

Now, if it is hard to imagine Rorty attaching such a qualification to his own ideas, this is because the act of uttering becomes vastly more problematic when understood from an antifoundational point of view. Patricia Bizzell, as noted earlier, wonders if undertaking a "positive assertion of the good" is even possible for antifoundational critics and teachers. In the presence of our students, Bizzell observes, "we exercise authority over them by asking them to give up their foundational beliefs, but we give them nothing to put in place of these foundational beliefs because we deny the validity of all authority, including, presumably, our own" (670). Even Rorty himself admits to certain brands of silence peculiar to antifoundationalist speakers. In considering what might possibly be said to those who commit any variety of atrocities, Rorty is all too aware of some rather serious constraints on how we address those whom, for reasons we believe just, we revile: "When the secret police come, when the torturers violate the innocent, there is nothing to be said to them of the form, 'There is something within you which you are betraying. Though you embody the practices of a totalitarian society which will endure forever, there is something beyond those practices which condemns you.'" Indeed, all of our objections, Rorty says, are freighted with a certain irony, an enlightened awareness that we can appeal to nothing transcendent, nothing beyond our historically-situated position, which, of course, we may vigorously defend or promote, but which has no force beyond our present contingencies. Such a position, as morally compromised as it must, Rorty admits, "is hard to live with" (*Consequences* xlii).

Returning to Bakhtin, I want to suggest a very different irony: if, as Bakhtin maintains, the superaddressee is a constituent aspect of the utterance, then Rorty's conversation owes a rather large debt to the ultimate contexts that it has repudiated. Or, to put this a bit differently, a sense of Edenic otherness, a sense of theory, makes possible the very conversation that denies the usefulness of theory and the ultimate contexts that theory (as a sense of theory) is able to offer. A conversation utterly bereft of superaddressees is not one that has divested itself of all unseemly idealism; it is one that has abandoned history and the temporal sense of experience. For such a conversation has foreclosed on Eden, has denied to its participants *a necessary elsewhere*, and, in so doing, has curtailed the possibility of better understandings, deeper commitments, more promising visions.

Bakhtin's requisite third party, I believe, offers a third way out, a convenient loophole through the impasse that constitutes the theory wars. His move to subsume theory into living, dialogic relations tries to preserve something of theory's historical charge—namely, to challenge the tyranny of the present by offering Edenic contexts within which greater understanding is possible. But this subsumptive move is also intended to challenge one of theory's traditional claims—that is, its putative ability to explain life from a position outside of life's living. The superaddressee may be read as Bakhtin's attempt to demonstrate the monologic tendencies of both theoretism *and* pragmatism, to reveal how it is that, while we may be wise to rid ourselves of theory, life without a sense of theory would be profoundly diminished, if not unsayable.

TWO THOUGHTS FOR THE WRITING CLASSROOM

Most of the foregoing discussion will probably seem at a considerable remove from our professional concerns as writing teachers, not to mention the everyday, prosaic concerns of our students. Rarefied, often obscure debates about foundationalism and antifoundationalism, as well as rarefied discussions of certain Bakhtinian texts, would hardly seem, on the face of things, to have any bearing whatsoever on what we do in our writing classrooms. But I would like to suggest otherwise. If one consequence of our antifoundational moment is that we have made assertion more difficult than ever or if we have burdened our students' utterances with the sorts of ironies that diminish their ability to say anything at all, then we should well expect to hear the presence of a superaddressee in their texts. In fact, I wish to argue that the superaddressee is very much an "invisibly present third party" (*SG* 126) in the texts that students write for us in composition classes—and, given some of the reasons outlined above, perhaps more so now than ever before. Let me close, then, by illustrating two contrasting ways that the superaddressee is likely to be manifested in our students' texts.

First, any reluctance to treat student texts as genuine utterances may result in our students writing for superaddressee audiences that do not include us at all. There can, of course, be any number of reasons why we could be perceived by students as having a tin ear toward their texts. We may, for example, be so scrupulously attuned to the formalities of their prose that we simply do not hear what they have to say. Or it may be that we devise assignments whose only seeming purpose is to supply us with school writing, "exercise" texts whose sole meaning resides in our evaluation of their merit. These are admittedly extreme illustrations, but I would caution that the student who becomes convinced of our inability to hear what he or she has to say will be understandably frustrated with, confused by, maybe even contemptuous of our efforts. That particular student, in other words, will likely be searching for a more perfect understanding than one we can provide. The student would likely either turn away from us as potentially responsive addressees of any sort and thus abandon any notion that what they write *for* us could be meaningful *to* us, or they would seek out other contexts for writing wherein some meaningful response might still be possible: letters, diaries, writing for friends or other classes, perhaps writing for other purposes of which we have no knowledge.

On the other hand, a markedly different situation emerges when we, as teachers, are invoked by our students as the superaddressee of their choice. Who has not encountered that student for whom the teacher serves the function of a superaddressee, that student perhaps reluctant to share his or her work with other students in peer workshops, but desperate to share with us some private concern, some intimacy, some achingly personal revelation? Often these confidences occur within the context of our classroom purposes—our discussions, readings, assignments, and so on; sometimes they do not. But as experienced teachers know, they inevitably occur, and we will have many occasions as teachers when we find ourselves invoked as a sympathetic third party for those students who, for whatever reasons, need a listener beyond the one defined by our pedagogical role in the institution.

But what happens when these two alternatives occur simultaneously? What happens, for example, when a student perceives us to be the greatest impediment to a fair hearing and, at the same time, the most likely candidate to provide one? What happens when we are constructed as adversary and ally, encumbrance and friend? In the next chapter, I will try to show how such doubling can occur within the writing of one student, Devlyn, who discovered a creative way to approach his rhetorical predicament.

2 AESOPIAN PREDICAMENTS, or BITING MY TONGUE AS I WRITE: *A Defense of Rhetorical Ambiguity*

Over a decade has passed since the appearance of Peter Elbow's essay, "Closing My Eyes As I Speak: A Plea for Ignoring Audience." In the years since its first publication, Elbow's article has been cited, praised, disparaged by some, but generally acknowledged as an important counterstatement to a good deal of then-current thinking about audience.

Elbow's article proceeds from what he calls a "limited claim," his view that "even though ignoring audience will usually lead to weak writing at first . . . this weak writing can help us in the end to better writing than we would have written if we'd kept readers in mind from the start" (51). Audiences, Elbow maintains, typically get in the way, interfere with our struggles to discover what it is we want to say, especially at the point when our thinking is inchoate and tentative about its ultimate direction. Yet, despite a title that might suggest otherwise, Elbow's argument is not for ignoring audience completely. Once we "have figured out our thinking . . . perhaps finding the right voice or stance as well," Elbow allows, "*then* we can . . . think about readers." A sequence emerges, then—one that accommodates a salutary disregard for our audience, followed by a scrupulous heeding of all such "traditional rhetorical advice" that requires us to take audience into account (52).

Elbow also recognizes that certain audiences—those he calls "inviting" or "enabling" audiences—may very well be "helpful to keep in mind from the start." But clearly his first interest is in those audiences who disturb our ability to write anything at all, listeners and readers whom Elbow refers to as "inhibiting" audiences. These are composed of "that person who intimidates us" or those "people who make us feel dumb when we try to speak to them" (51) or even such "readers with whom we have an awkward relationship" (52). Indeed, for Elbow, it goes without saying that inhibiting audiences are, by definition, impediments to a writer's struggle to say something authentic and compelling to others. But they are something else too.

Notice that, in Elbow's descriptions, inhibiting audiences are almost always personal, immediate, overwhelmingly present. Inhibiting audiences, in other words, are made up of "that person" or "of people" or (in educational contexts) of individual teachers, classmates, and proximate adults. When Elbow gets around to suggesting that certain, more general audiences might also be inhibiting, he mentions only those audiences that would appear nowhere else but in (not especially inspired) writing assignments—audiences such as "the general public" and "educated readers" (52). Whatever intimidating force these larger audiences might have, it seems to originate not from any implied danger or threat that might be unleashed, but rather from the sheer vagueness of who these audiences are.

A second matter for which Elbow does not show much concern is the possibility of *resisting* those audiences that inhibit or intimidate. Elbow does not extend much consideration to how it might be possible to subvert or possibly circumvent an inhibiting audience, how it might be that we are able to overcome an inhibiting audience in order to reach an intended, secondary audience. True, Elbow will concede that writers sometimes find themselves having to *disguise* their point of view. But that fact alone doesn't exempt the writer from the need to ignore audience, because, as Elbow points out, "it's hard to disguise something while engaged in the process of trying to figure it out" (52).

Elbow, moreover, acknowledges the problem of what he calls "double audiences," those audiences constituted of two readerships: for example, a memo sent both to colleagues and to a supervisor; a submitted article that must satisfy the demands both of editors and of readers; and, perhaps most relevant to my purposes here, a student paper written supposedly for a designated "real world" audience, but understood by every student to be written "really" for the teacher. Indeed, Elbow concludes by asking us to consider the obvious: namely, the possibility that we teachers might represent both an enabling and inhibiting audience for our students.

In the pages to follow, I elaborate on a number of these ideas, developing those points that receive not much more than passing mention by Elbow. In particular, I point out how inhibiting audiences can and do surpass the merely personal and immediate, even when it may seem that such audiences are located exclusively within those domains. Moreover, I show how what Elbow calls disguised writing can be illuminated through the prism of intellectual and literary traditions in Russian letters, wherein a certain kind of disguised writing can be understood as a strategy for creative resistance to powerful audiences that not only inhibit, but inhibit in ways that could prove injurious or even fatal to the writer. I then return to the classroom to examine the far less violent (but no less real) predicament—I will call it an "Aesopian" predicament—of one writer and the particular strategies he uses to disguise and confound his purposes for an audience that he perceives to be threatening.

AESOPIANISM IN THE RUSSIAN TRADITION

Aesopianism is a term that has emerged fairly recently in much of the secondary literature about Bakhtin and his circle. Michael Gardiner, in his *Dialogics of Critique,* attributes the origin of the term to the Soviet scholar Boris Kagarlitsky, who describes a Aesopian the general condition of the Russian intelligentsia roughly from the period of 1917-1940, a time characterized by enormous social upheaval followed by state-enforced repression and terror. As explained by Gardiner, because writers and intellectuals could not "address pressing contemporary political and social issues directly," they were forced to develop alternate ways of writing and speaking—or, to be more precise, *allegorical* strategies for communicating with each other while, at the same time, escaping the notice of censors and various state agents and bureaucrats. Gardiner observes, for example, that an Aesopian approach to social and political matters resulted in such problems being discussed under camouflage, that is, under the precarious cover of acceptable cultural and literary forms (232, n. 37).

Caryl Emerson, on the other hand, claims that Aesopian language—or rather, the need for Aesopian language—has been something of a constant of Russian discourse for nearly a millennium:

For most of Russian culture . . . the printed word was viewed as sacred,
and it was, in varying degrees, unfree. To outwit the unfree authoritarian
word, numerous strategies were developed in the nineteenth century—
among them "Aesopian language," a hermeneutic device perfected by
Russia's radical intelligentsia. Designed to work under combat conditions,
Aesopianism assumes that the word is allegory, that no one speaks or
writes straight, and that every officially public or published text (by definition censored) has a "more honest," multilayered, hidden subtext that
only insiders can decode. . . . Russia's greatest writers have been alert to the
dangers of Aesopian thinking and at the same time fairly drawn to indulge
in it. In the words of two prominent American students of Russian contemporary culture, Russian literary language was "the antithesis of 'plain-
speak'; instead it was a kind of culturally institutionalized and revered
'oblique-speak.'" (*First* 8-9)

Emerson goes on to observe that honest, critical ideas sought and
found refuge in literary discourse. For at least the last century and a
half, she argues, "Russian readers were trained to see nonfunctional
referents beneath every fictional surface" (*First* 9). Thus, in Russia, literary ascendancy in both artistic and critical genres *mattered* in ways
that American writers of the same period might not have been able to
fathom. As Emerson points out, literary accomplishment, while desirable, was nevertheless an extremely hazardous business. To be blunt,
"you could get arrested and killed for it" (10). And yet, at the same
time, literary artistry and criticism offered the best venues for dissem-
inating serious, critical ideas in disguised forms.

And what does this Aesopian milieu tell us about the life and times
of Mikhail Bakhtin?

I believe that Aesopian requirements permeated most of Bakhtin's
thinking and likewise determined a good many events of his life. For
example, we know that, in an interview with Sergei Bocharov conducted toward the end of Mikhail Bakhtin's life, he insisted that he was
first and foremost a philosopher and that his "turn" toward literary
criticism, if one can call it that, was occasioned by pressures that could
only be called Aesopian. Thus, when asked about his relatively uncon-
troversial *Problems of Dostoevsky's Poetics,* Bakhtin declared his bril-
liant work to be "morally flawed." When further pressed as to what he

meant, Bakhtin replied, "The way I could have written it would have been very different from the way it is. After all, in that book, I severed form from the main thing. I couldn't speak directly about the main questions." Bocharov then asked: "What main questions, M. M.?" "Philosophical questions," Bakhtin answered. "In the [Dostoevsky] book I was constantly forced to prevaricate, to dodge backward and forward. I had to hold back constantly. The moment a thought got going, I had to break it off. Backward and forward" (1012).

Bocharov reports that Bakhtin was, on the whole, rather dismissive of his contributions as a literary critic and historian and that, moreover, Bakhtin deeply regretted that he could not broach philosophical questions in a directly philosophical manner.[1] Though literary criticism may indeed have provided Bakhtin with a mask that he donned reluctantly, it also provided him with a new way to think about Dostoevsky, a way that departed profoundly from rather entrenched traditions of Russian philosophical criticism. More than that, Bocharov further suggests that the fact "that he [Bakhtin] was unfree to think philosophically 'about the main questions' directly" may have resulted in his discovery of dialogue not only as "the inner form of the novel," but likewise as the single, overarching theme with which his work has become identified. "Surely," Bocharov adds, "we don't need to regret this achievement" (1020).

But just as surely, Bocharov notes, we need to recognize that Bakhtin did indeed regret, if not the achievement, then the decision to compromise his inclinations. And yet who could fully resist the Aesopian call and its ethically questionable demands? "Everything that was created during this past half century," Bakhtin laments, "on this graceless soil, beneath this unfree sky, all of it is to some degree morally flawed" (1012).

Of course, many of the controversies surrounding the authorship of the disputed texts must be understood in light of Aesopian requirements as well. Whether or not, or to what extent, Bakhtin authored or co-authored texts signed by his contemporaries, V. N. Volosinov and Pavel Medvedev, it remains clear that the severe hazards of publication in those times had no small influence on how the word—Bakhtin's word—was disseminated. After reporting Bakhtin's admission that he wrote much of the disputed material, Bocharov quotes Bakhtin as saying that "publications not in my name were acceptable." Bocharov then explains,

> [H]e could speak out, but only from perspectives that he would not adopt under his name. Evidently, this strange form of cooperation suited his friends as well, who accepted (or proposed) it. "M. M., in your own name you would have written differently," I asked him on 10 April 1974. "Yes, I would have." (1015).

Bakhtin's admission, of course, does not resolve the many complexities of the authorship question. And, as Bocharov is quick to point out, "even Bakhtin's personal testimony is not enough to decide the question," especially for those scholars who continue to demand "incontrovertible proof" (1014). Yet surely, if Bakhtin (and Bocharov) are to be believed—and there is no reason to doubt either—then Bakhtin's pseudonymous ventures must be understood not only as helpful gestures to close associates, but also as strategies by which he could simultaneously disguise and circulate his ideas.

And what of those ideas? Does Aesopianism in any way shape not merely the conditions and forms of his thought, but the content of it as well? To my knowledge, no thorough examination of the Aesopian influences on Bakhtin's ideas has been undertaken. But surely there is ample warrant for such an analysis, especially since Aesopian requirements were so relentlessly pervasive in the culture in which he wrote. I will mention two examples where it seems likely that Aesopianism had a determining influence on his thought.

First, and perhaps most obviously, Bakhtin's analysis of double-voicing in Dostoevsky's novels undoubtedly had its analogues in the larger culture in which both Dostoevsky and Bakhtin wrote. In his charting of double-voiced discourses presented in the Dostoevsky book, Bakhtin catalogues a variety of double-voiced forms, the most compelling of which are those that fall under the title of "active double-voiced discourse." Here, among other possibilities, Bakhtin introduces us to what he calls "hidden polemic," or "internally polemical discourse," a particular species of double-voicing that he also refers to metaphorically as the "word with a sideward glance." Internally polemical discourse, Bakhtin observes, always casts a sideward glance at "someone else's hostile word." "Here," Bakhtin tells us, "belong, in everyday speech, all words that 'make digs at others' and all 'barbed' words. But here also belongs all self-deprecating overblown speech that repudiates itself in advance, speech with a thousand reservations, concessions, loopholes, and the like" (*PDP* 196). In other words, hidden polemic is wholly shaped by an anticipation of how it will be received, and, as a consequence, stakes its position (caviling, accommodating, qualifying, etc.) toward its anticipated reception. What it simply cannot afford to do is forget those who will receive it, the presumed others to whom it owes its special construction.

Of course, we admire Bakhtin for the insights he brings to bear on the kinds of double-voicing that occur between characters and between author and character in Dostoevsky's novels. But we may just as well admire these insights as a description of the conditions under which Bakhtin and many of his contemporaries were forced to write. After all, in Aesopian contexts, one had better not risk leaving home, so to speak, without a sure and steady supply of "sideward glances," especially if one hopes to survive, much less be heard. Bakhtin, in my view, understood that double-voicing went far beyond the limits of the novel and that it was a concept that could usefully describe the cultural and political exigencies of publication during these times.

A second, likely example of how Aesopian requirements entered into the substance of Bakhtin's work can be discovered in his theme of carnival. Here, certain scholars have indeed examined the Aesopian dimensions of the carnival theme and, in particular, the work where it finds its most thorough elaboration, *Rabelais and His World*. In their biography of Bakhtin, Katrina Clark and Michael Holquist read Bakhtin's carnival theme as a veiled critique of Stalinist repression and what Bakhtin perceived to be the hierarchical imposition of a "'vertical world' of absolute values" (308). Bakhtin's carnival writings, with their famous celebration of "joyful relativity," stand as a guise by which to confront the monologic seriousness of Stalin's power:

> Thus, in a time of increasing regimentation, Bakhtin wrote of freedom. In a time of authoritarianism, dogmatism, and official culture, he wrote of the masses as ebullient, variegated, and irreverent. At a time when literature was

composed of mandated canons, he wrote of smashing all norms and canons, and ridiculed the pundits who upheld them. At a time when everyone was told to "look higher" and to deny the body and its dictates, he extolled the virtues of the everyday, and advocated reveling in the basic functions of what he called the "lower bodily stratum." (312)

How, then, could Bakhtin possibly get away with what would seem to most a transparent attack on the prevailing regime? According to Clark and Holquist, Bakhtin was able to make his points "palatable by an adroit use of Aesopian language and allegory" (312). Again, the genre of literary criticism provided Bakhtin with a vehicle for criticizing social and political repression in a disguised manner. In the literary context of the Rabelais work, the fount of social repression and official culture is not to be identified ostensibly with Stalin, but rather with the Roman Catholic Church, a predictable enemy for Stalinist dogma. Clark and Holquist add that Bakhtin consistently "exploited the device of ambiguity," and that he often borrowed certain stock clichés from official discourses, making certain that his carnival thesis, moreover, had already found authoritative expression in the work of approved writers, such as Maxim Gorky and party functionary, Anatoly Lunacharsky. Thus, Clark and Holquist conclude that in the Rabelais book, as elsewhere, Bakhtin deployed a strategy that he found particularly useful. He would borrow "the ideas and rhetoric of his age," Clark and Holquist observe, and use "them to his own ends." Yet importantly, they are quick to add, "he co-opts only those elements that can in some way be made to approximate his own views" (312-14).

What's clear from this discussion is that Bakhtin's works and days were marked by Aesopian requirements, by a tacitly understood need for the act of saying to be disguised, elusive, resisting, allegorical, confounding—all of these, in fact, if the word, especially the published word, was to be heard by those for whom it was intended.

AESOPIANISM IN THE WRITING CLASSROOM

Do our students ever sense the need to disguise their opinions, to write in a purposely oblique, deflective manner as a strategy by which to voice their resistance to what we teach? Do they ever choose, in other words, to write in ways that salvage a measure of honest expression, yet simultaneously escape the institutional penalties that accrue to school culture in general and to the individual teacher in particular?

At the outset of this section, I hope it is obvious to readers that I do not plan to suggest an equivalence between the Aesopian circumstances faced by Bakhtin and the ones faced by our students. Those distinct circumstances do not compare—either in their historical moments or their cultural ubiquity or the severity of their consequences. For these reasons, there would be no warrant for attempting to draw an equivalence between the conditions under which Bakhtin wrote and those under which our students write. But there may be some value in exploring an analogy—a limited analogy, to be sure— but one founded upon a shared need *to utter truly* under circumstances that are perceived to be hazardous for doing so. Bakhtin and our students have in common at least this much.

Yet how do we know that our students possess an awareness that writing is a tricky business, a matter fraught with dangers, traps, unexpected snares, assorted humiliations, and, not least, a host of what are often thought to be punitive consequences?

We know this from what they tell us. What experienced teacher, for example, has not heard from that student who, in tones of utter despair and sometimes anger, implores the teacher to "just tell me what you want?" The student who voices this plea is one who has surrendered to the institutional authority of school and its most immediate representative, the teacher. Such a student has simply given up any illusion that what she writes for class might somehow reflect her life, her values, opinions, feelings, thoughts, and so on. Unfortunately, such a student has abandoned as well the possibility that there might be ways to circumvent what she perceives to be an impossible situation. Or, to put the matter baldly, that there might be ways to satisfy the teacher and, at the same time, exercise some fidelity to one's own words—to have one's say without inviting reprisals in the form of, among other sanctions, lower grades. Still, at the opposite end of the spectrum, we may just as well ask: what teacher has not encountered that student who is apparently intent on resisting everything we say, everything we teach, and everything we require of our classes?

I first met Devlyn three years ago.[2] He had enrolled in my Advanced Composition class and during the first week of the semester, Devlyn made an unforgettable impression both upon his classmates and upon me. Devlyn seemed to me then, as now, to be extremely bright, charming, energetic, funny, chiding, socially conservative, and unrelentingly argumentative. Among his classmates, I had the impression that Devlyn was, more than anything else, indulged. I sensed that many of the other students were uncomfortable with Devlyn's intensity in our class discussions and the sheer earnestness with which he spoke. Perhaps his classmates felt Devlyn's manner to be merely off-putting, but I am inclined to think that Devlyn was seen as a threat to something less obvious. To be more precise, Devlyn represented an unwelcome disruption to that atmosphere of genteel non-involvement that some students come to expect and, indeed, depend upon. Devlyn, in other words, upped the verbal ante for his classmates. It was not hard for me to imagine any number of his classmates saying to themselves, "If this guy speaks so passionately about his views, must I do so as well?"

One student, however, had no reticence whatsoever in speaking with comparable passion. Unfortunately, her passion seemed to be directed toward Devlyn and not course materials. Mary Beth was a returning student who had come back to school to pursue a degree in English Education. She hoped to become certified to teach middle school, and my course was part of her degree requirements. What was *not* part of her requirements, I gathered from her later comments, was that she would be asked to put up with someone like Devlyn. After listening in silence to my increasingly frequent—and, I would add, uncomfortable—jousting with Devlyn, Mary Beth had had enough. She finally gave vent to her anger at Devlyn, and not surprisingly, he responded in kind. Before long, their skirmishes became legendary, at least among classmates. Moreover, their disputes also became more personal, until I was forced to do something I had not done in any other class: I enforced a verbal cease-fire between the two antagonists—much to the relief of their classmates, I was later informed. I came to see that, notwithstanding what I had thought was a commitment to open, free exchange in the classroom, I had allowed a very unproductive situation to go on far too long.

But what exactly was it that provoked these outbursts of classroom ferocity? As I look back, it seems that Mary Beth's vehemence was largely a response to Devlyn, and Devlyn's was, for the most part, a response to the assigned readings and class discussions. In particular, what annoyed Devlyn was our first reading of the semester, Paulo Freire's "The Banking Concept of Education," from our required text, Bartholomae and Petrosky's *Ways of Reading* (3rd ed.). Freire's essay was one of three that made up our first unit, "The Aims of Education"; the other two selections were Richard Rodriguez's "The Achievement of Desire" and Adrienne Rich's "When We Dead Awaken." Devlyn didn't much care for these latter two either, but it was Freire who seemed most to provoke his sense of outrage.

As our class made its way through the many difficulties of Freire's essay, it became clear that Devlyn disagreed with each and every concept that Freire introduces in this selection—the very notion of a "banking concept of education," the annoying fuzziness of what Freire means by problem-posing education, the idea of teachers and students as "critical co-investigators," the political importance of *conscientização*, and the implied value of teaching circles as a method for adult literacy education. On all of these points, Devlyn voiced his uncompromising disagreements, his forceful arguments usually directed toward me, but occasionally toward other students, fending off, in particular, the likewise forceful comments of his nemesis, Mary Beth.

I wondered if—or perhaps how—the fervor of these class discussions might appear in Devlyn's formal writing for the unit. I already had a good idea of what I was likely to read in his journal, since we began each class with a journal prompt that often served to frame the discussion for that day. But I had *no* idea of what Devlyn would do with an assignment that called upon him to recontextualize Freire's ideas. Here's a shortened version of the first assignment for this unit:

> Consider a recent event in your life which you found, in some way, oppressive, and which you believe exemplifies the "banking" concept as it might be confronted in everyday, "real" life. Your description of this event or situation will constitute the first part of your essay. Then, using the idea of problem-posing education as a tool, analyze your experience from a Freirean perspective. Note, however, that your particular experience need

not be one which occurred in the classroom or as part of your formal education. Your purpose is to apply Freire's ideas to your personal experience, and your audience is Dr. Farmer.

Withholding my comments for the time being, I offer below Devlyn's response (in full) to this assignment.

Oppression for the Opposition, Please

When this essay was assigned, we (your humble students) were asked to recount a recent experience that we found to be "oppressive." We were also asked to include examples of Freire's "banking" concept, and show how these events followed the same path as Freire's ideas. After reading the assignment sheet with despair, I raised my hand looking to Dr. Farmer for relief. I proceeded to ask if someone (read: *me*) had a problem with Freire's ideology, were they to put that aside and write the paper as if they agreed with him. Dr. Farmer's bemused answer was, yes, for the sake of the assignment, follow the directions to the letter. Disgruntled, I left the room with the arduous task of applying some event in my life to a set of criteria I didn't even BELIEVE in. Then, it hit me . . . asking me to write a paper that adheres to Freire's ideas without questioning them is, in essence, both *banking* and *oppressive!* Anxiously, I reread Freire to gather the support for this idea.

In the "banking" concept of education, Freire reveals that "the scope of action allowed to the students extends only as far as receiving, filing, and storing the deposits." When Freire's essay was first brought up for debate in the classroom, I vehemently rebuffed his ideas and dismissed them as "touchy-feely" liberalism. My attitudes towards Freire's concepts, although unpopular with the majority of my classmates, were allowed to stand on their own. Freire would have been proud, I believe, that I wasn't asked to receive the information, consider it to be fact unquestioningly, and then regurgitate it later for proving I learned the material. What I think Freire would have found oppressive is the fact that when the assignment was brought to light, I was asked to abandon my opposing viewpoint, and simply *concede* to what was being taught and then apply it to my own life. This eliminates my critical co-investigation skills when I'm not left to explore any viewpoint but what's already been written. The option wasn't given to write a paper AGAINST Freire's ideas, only to support them. I learned Freire, remembered Freire, spit him back up without challenging the authority of the teacher. The "banking" result is this paper.

I considered going against the grain and writing a paper on "Why I Dislike Freire's Ideas," but I realized that when Dr. Farmer told me that I was to put my own ideology and opinion aside, this strengthened Freire's concept of the oppressor's behaviors. Freire states that when a teacher or authority figure "chooses and enforces his choice, and the students comply," that is considered oppressive. Dr. Farmer told me that I had to follow the guidelines even though I didn't like them, and I did. That, according to Freire is oppression. Freire also contends that when teachers simply choose the content to be pored over without consulting the students, it's the mark of the oppressor. I wasn't asked whether or not I wanted to read Freire, nor was I given a choice to write this paper supporting Freire without being punished. Dr. Farmer, in his syllabus nonetheless, informs his students that all of his assignments must be completed "in order for you to pass this course." In Freire's eyes, Dr. Farmer could not be seen as anything *but* an oppressor. An oppressor who has told his students, by way of threatening to fail them, that they must do things as he has laid out for them. The result of these commands is this paper, a jumble of non-authentic thoughts.

Freire states that most oppressors don't see themselves as such. I think Dr. Farmer should be made aware of his oppressions, and be helped to change his ways. Perhaps on the next assignment Dr. Farmer should allow more dialogue and flexibility between student and professor. Freire contends that in true problem-posing education, Dr. Farmer should present "the material to the students for their consideration, and then reconsider his earlier considerations as *the students express their own*." I think Freire makes a very good point. Teachers should readjust their priorities, assignments, and readings to the liking of their students. That way, students wouldn't have to endure the evils that professors inflict upon them, which we might never have known about unless Freire taught us about them, right?

To recap, this entire paper was an exercise in oppression, which was created by an oppressor, to oppress me and make sure that I could regurgitate Freire if I HAD to. After playing up Freire's ideas and concepts on education for three pages, I think it's only fair that I end the paper by making this point. I don't believe a word I said.

After my initial reading of this paper, my first inclination was to return it to Devlyn and ask that it be rewritten according to the requirements of the assignment. In particular, I was bothered by the scant attention given to problem-posing education—even though other students, too, had a difficult time paraphrasing what Freire meant by this term. I was also bothered by Devlyn's handling of audience. Because this was the first assignment of the term, I had designated myself as the intended audience, believing that Devlyn and his classmates would be both well-practiced and comfortable with having to write for their teacher. Even though from this point in the semester we moved into more distant and complex audiences, it seemed appropriate that for the first assignment, I name myself as primary audience.

Now, apart from the *ad hominem* quality of Devlyn's discussion, what bothered me most was his choice to refer to his audience in the third person. Thus, Devlyn informs us that "Dr. Farmer told me I was to put my own ideology aside" and that "Dr. Farmer should be made aware of his oppressions" and so on. It seemed odd to address his specified audience, me, in the third person. An obvious question arose then: to whom are these words addressed? Surely, one of composition's most durable truisms is that audiences are always, in some measure, constructions. But is it possible that the same audience may be doubly constructed? This is exactly what I sensed in Devlyn's essay—the presence of two Dr. Farmers, one spoken *to*, the other spoken *of*. In Bakhtin's terms, the person referred to as "Dr. Farmer" is the hero of Devlyn's discourse, its central theme to which Devlyn is oriented in an obviously evaluative way.[4] But the other Dr. Farmer, the one actually reading Devlyn's essay, it would seem, is enlisted as an ally who will stand alongside Devlyn in his many grievances against the named "Dr. Farmer" who appears in his essay. Again, using Bakhtinian terms, we might be tempted to say that Dr. Farmer, the reader, constitutes a *superaddressee* audience for Devlyn, an ideal but necessary third party, who will be responsive to his complaints, his request for the sort of fair hearing that Dr. Farmer, the teacher, could not or would not provide.

Of course, yet *another* Dr. Farmer—the one writing this book—did not respond warmly to Devlyn's representations, at least not after a first reading. To be called an "oppressor," not once but on several occasions throughout Devlyn's essay, was admittedly a bit hard to take, especially when one doesn't usually see oneself that way, as Devlyn (citing Freire) is quick to point out. Nothing too earth-shattering about that, I suppose. Nevertheless, after recovering from the initial sting of Devlyn's words, I resolved not to react—or overreact—to the personal, *ad hominem* features of his essay, but to try to understand what Devlyn was doing, to fathom why he decided to write *this paper this way.*

Simply put, what I determined was that Devlyn had something clear and forceful to say, but that his judgments about his teacher, about our particular class, about the rules, niceties, conventions, and habits of the institution—all of these, in fact, required Devlyn to be elusive and confounding in the manner of his saying. Elusive? Confounding? On a surface reading, it would seem that Devlyn's essay is nothing but straightforward—brutally direct, as a matter of fact, at least within certain passages. How could it possibly be argued that his paper seeks to elude the one reader it most desires to confront? How could it be said, in other words, that Devlyn's writing is Aesopian?

My earliest written response to Devlyn's essay tries to point out these contradictory tendencies or at least to show him the confusions I experienced while reading his paper. At the bottom of the paragraph that closes with "a jumble of non-authentic thoughts," I questioned Devlyn about his intended meaning(s):

> Hmmm . . . You seem to be saying that this protest against my banking methods is "a jumble of non-authentic thoughts." Does that mean that you don't really believe that I'm a banking teacher, or that Freire is way off base? I don't find your essay jumbled or insincere, though only you could know the latter.

I was obviously struck by that phrase, "a jumble of non-authentic thoughts." Confused by this admission, I wondered to which of Devlyn's statements his seemingly blanket disclaimer was meant to apply. Given the positions he assumed in class, it was not hard to understand why Devlyn would consider the requirement of having to draw upon Freire for argumentative support as "non-authentic." He was no doubt miffed that the assignment forced him to write from a

Freirean point of view, or, in Bakhtinian terms, in a voice that he unequivocally rejected, indeed loathed. But notice that Devlyn's efforts to invalidate his statements are not limited to what Freire has to say. In fact, Devlyn tells his reader that it is *"this paper"* (my emphasis) that constitutes a "jumble of non-authentic thoughts." Would that not, then, include his condemnations of Dr. Farmer? When Devlyn says that "Dr. Farmer should be made aware of his oppressions," am I to read that statement as an authentic or non-authentic expression of Devlyn's views? And what if I choose to read Devlyn's unflattering judgments of Dr. Farmer as insincere or "inauthentic"? Would that not mean, oddly enough, that Devlyn approves of the banking methods that, in Devlyn's view, I (hypocritically) embrace?

My confusions did not get clarified in the remainder of the paper, nor did my uneasiness abate. In fact, by the end of his essay, when Devlyn closes with that magisterial final sentence, "I don't believe a word I said," I was more baffled—and, I should add—more deflated than ever. What teacher, after all, would be pleased at this confession of dishonesty? True, as before, that final sentence could be interpreted to mean that Devlyn doesn't believe a single word or idea he appropriated from Freire for the task of writing this paper. But could it not also mean that Devlyn didn't believe any of those *other* words either, the ones he used to convey his rather severe judgments of Dr. Farmer? And if the latter possibility is true, doesn't Devlyn's last sentence amount to a sort of "just kidding" close to a paper that in every other moment seems to relish lambasting his teacher for inconsistencies and "oppressions"?

In my final comment of his paper, I once again drew attention to the perplexities I experienced as a reader.

Will the real Devlyn please stand up? This is a smart, creative, and well-written response to the assignment. One of the keys to understanding your paper is uncovering the central assumption upon which it is based, namely, that because Dr. Farmer assigns Freire, he must therefore agree with everything Freire says. I wonder. . . . The confusing thing is where *you* stand on the issues you raise. You make a very strong (and insightful) critique of your teacher (on behalf of your "real" views), and then you tell me those aren't the real views you hold. Baffling.

I once again found myself struggling to make sense of yet another of Devlyn's grand, sweeping comments, a statement whose only apparent purpose was to invalidate everything else he said. My end comment reiterates my confusion, but with something of a reflexive twist. I tried to call Devlyn's attention to what I think to be the single guiding assumption of his paper, one that basically says that because a teacher teaches Freire, he or she must agree with Freire. I wanted Devlyn to entertain the notion that it might be possible to think *with* Freire, to write *with* Freire, to teach *with* Freire, and yet not to surrender oneself completely to Freire's ideas. Indeed, I hoped to nudge Devlyn into considering that he just might become a *better* critic of Freire if he agreed (however briefly) to place himself inside of Freire's perspective. I wanted Devlyn to know that positioning himself with Freire need not involve a compromise of his integrity. In short, I thought if I could establish the conditions for Devlyn and his classmates to make Freire "their own," or in Bakhtin's now familiar terms, to make Freire something of an "internally persuasive discourse" instead of an "authoritative" one, then I had, in some small measure, accomplished the important pedagogical goal of bringing close an otherwise remote and difficult text (*DI* 341-42). I wanted to give my students the opportunity to wrangle with, contend with, struggle with Freire. Indeed, my assignment was designed with this sole purpose in mind.

These intentions for Devlyn and his classmates were admittedly self-serving. When I teach Paulo Freire—or Adrienne Rich, Walker Percy, Richard Rodriguez, Joyce Carol Oates, and others—I customarily present their respective texts *in voice,* as if I were ventriloquizing their perspectives. In my experience, I have discovered this method to be more provocative of classroom dialogue than, say, disclosure approaches wherein teachers announce their social and political stances, their opinions of particular texts, and so on to their students. In my experience, such disclosures have something of a chilling effect, often eliciting more silence than vigorous engagement, more parroting of teacher's views than honest discernment.

But, then, doesn't Devlyn prove me wrong on this point? Indeed, in retrospect, it seems to me that Devlyn was invigorated by the prospect that my teaching of Freire was somehow a full disclosure of my endorsement of Freire's views. As I note in my end comment, Devlyn concludes that because I chose to teach Freire and that because I spent a good deal of time explicating Freire's concepts, I must wholeheartedly embrace Freire's views. Otherwise, that "gotcha" quality to his writing would not be so sharp, so pronounced. (As a matter of fact, there is much in Freire that I do endorse, but there are facets of his work that I question and find rather off-putting.) And yet the Dr. Farmer constructed by Devlyn in his essay is clearly someone who is an enthusiast, a true believer, a devotee to a Freirean worldview.

What Devlyn does not allow himself, or me, is the possibility of some middle ground on the issues raised by Freire. For Devlyn, the requirement to write *with* Freire, even temporarily, could involve nothing but a compromise of his own viewpoint, his very integrity. The problem he faced then was how to give expression to his point of view, and, at the same time, satisfy what the assignment called for. More than that, he had to accomplish this task in such a way that did not invite severe reprisals from his instructor. Devlyn, in other words, faced an Aesopian predicament and responded appropriately to his predicament with Aesopian strategies.

What sort of Aesopian strategies? As I earlier noted, Devlyn's essay can be read as one that constructs two audiences, two Dr. Farmers, one of whom he musters as an ally in his disagreements with the other. Recall that Dr. Farmer, the teacher, is something of a prop, a straw man, a foil, for Devlyn's vehemence, while the other Dr. Farmer, the one reading and evaluating Devlyn's essay, is, potentially at least, someone who could lend a sympathetic ear, someone who might be able to understand the predicament that Devlyn found himself in when faced with having to write this essay.

Had I been satisfied with a facile reading of his paper, I would have been content to dismiss Devlyn's words as the grumblings of a bright, clever, and fairly resentful student, apparently someone who, for whatever reason, was hell-bent on offending his teacher. But I heard in Devlyn's words other tones, beseeching and earnest tones, tones that sought out a fair hearing for his point of view, that sought some understanding beyond the diatribe that he presented to me. Whatever inclinations I had to be punitive in my response to Devlyn slowly faded as I came to realize that I had been doubly constructed as an audience, that I was for Devlyn both an enemy and a possible ally. I chose to be more of the latter toward Devlyn, a decision that marked our relationship throughout the remainder of the term.

As I also observed, Devlyn's essay is Aesopian because it periodically issues sweeping disclaimers, blanket statements whose apparent purpose is to invalidate everything else that has been said by its author. Although Devlyn seems to be most direct and clear when he divulges that his paper is "a jumble of non-authentic thoughts" or when he concludes with the sentence, "I don't believe a word I said," Devlyn is, in fact, at his most elusive and obscure. He ends up leaving his reader, *this* reader, thoroughly confused as to exactly where he stands. Was that what Devlyn wanted to do? Did he intend to befuddle? Confound? Evade? Did Devlyn devise a clever way to avoid being pinned down—a way that also served to exempt him from responsibility for his words?

I don't know. But I realized that, had I chosen to confront Devlyn about those somewhat personal accusations toward his teacher, I would have had a difficult time doing so. By making sure that he disavowed all that he asserted, Devlyn had effectively given himself a loophole (or in official parlance, "deniability"). Had I confronted Devlyn about the various accusations of "oppressions" that he leveled against me, he could simply deny that he ever intended his words to be read that way. After all, could he not justifiably remind me that he didn't believe *a word* of what he wrote?

If I read him correctly, Devlyn had found a way to make his point and, at the same time, protect himself against a harsh reprisal. Not that what he turned in entailed no risk whatsoever. It surely must have occurred to Devlyn that he might receive a failing grade or a demand that he rewrite the entire paper or, at the very least, a verbal reprimand of some kind. Such likely responses must have crossed his mind. But Devlyn chose to take a measured risk: using the words and concepts of a thinker he despised, Devlyn turned those same words and concepts against his teacher, the person who made him write an assignment that he found to be distasteful, "oppressive." More importantly, he took pains to minimize the risks involved by deploying the sorts of Aesopian strategies that I outline here. Devlyn received a high mark on this first paper. I liked the intellectual energy I sensed in reading his rather combative prose, however uncomfortable it was to encounter upon a first reading. I also liked the ingenuity with which he approached an assignment that he clearly did not want to write. More than anything, though, I liked how Devlyn had discovered a way to speak his piece yet do so in a manner that made teacherly sanctions difficult or unlikely. For this assignment, Devlyn proved himself to be a deft rhetorician, an Aesopian writer of no mean ability. Or, was it possible that I read too much into his paper?

In keeping with the dialogic purpose of this discussion, I asked Devlyn to answer my interpretation of his paper. I close with his response.

Looking Back, Three Years Later

When I arrived at East Carolina University, I was excited at the chance to finally write as an adult. I had endured the restraints of high school censorship for four years, and I was eager to push the buttons of any college professor I encountered. Whenever I was asked to compose a paper, I found myself purposefully trying to go against the spirit of the assignment but still fulfilling the requirements for it. My intention, honestly, was to see if I could be penalized for my views while still completing the work as instructed. It was innocent at first, slipping in curse words when I felt justified, personally insulting the subject(s) of the assignment, or using colorful but unnecessary analogies. I breezed my way through my freshman and sophomore courses, never receiving any criticism for the faux-fanaticism with which I approached my work.

This being said, I must admit that there were times when I really did not believe a word of what I wrote, because I was writing mostly to shock and elicit response from my instructors. Upon arriving in Dr. Farmer's Advanced Composition class, I fully intended to keep pushing until I was reprimanded. I envisioned the day when a teacher tried to censor or dock my grade because that teacher didn't agree with my opinion. I knew I could win that argument (I was very confrontational at that point in my schooling). Fortunately, I realized within a week of taking Dr. Farmer's course that I would not need to fabricate outrage, but would be supplied it on a class to class basis.

Dr. Farmer makes reference to Mary Beth, a woman with whom I had numerous heated discussions during class. When ideas and ideologies are being bandied about, I am not one to back down. Half of the situation was honest disbelief at what was being taught; the other half was playing devil's advocate. It was very rare for me to go to a class and actually have an intense discussion—more common was the uninterested silence that pervaded my lecture-based classes.

When the Freire assignment was first handed down, I was somewhat taken by surprise. I couldn't really believe the box that Dr. Farmer had constructed for himself. As someone who was dying to find conflict and "nail his teacher to the wall," so to speak, this absolutely overjoyed me. How, on the one hand, could Dr. Farmer actually teach Freire's ideology of educational freedom, then expect me to write a paper that would ultimately end with me using an experience from my own life to validate Freire's views? After receiving additional confirmation that this was what Dr. Farmer wanted, I strolled home along Tenth Street, relishing the almost certain conflict to come.

As I sat down at the computer to write what I felt at the time to be my most defiant masterpiece, I actually reconsidered it for a moment. Was this going too far? Attacking a teacher for doing his job? I wondered if it would just be simpler to do the assignment and let it go. After discussing Freire at length in class, and being verbally chastised by fellow classmates (at least that's how I saw it then), I knew there was no way that I was *not* going to write this paper.

I have always had a knack for manipulating words and ideas and turning them against people. I was absolutely dumbfounded at how Dr. Farmer could plant the seeds of Freire (with great fervor, I might add) in our minds, and then engage the very thing Freire discourages! I set out with the intention of writing a paper that would simply make him angry, but, as I found myself in the middle of my essay, I realized that I was actually making a valid point.

Teaching students about educational freedom obviously comes with many perils, the most basic being, "How do I teach someone *not* to merely receive the information as *I* see fit to dispense it?" It has been my experience that only the very exceptional student will go beyond the classroom and assigned readings to the point of actually having an "authentic" learning experience. Most students have a predisposition to simply learn the material well enough to pass the test, and then forget it. This pattern is bred from a continuous line of teachers who fail to inspire, and students who fail to care about their education. I think Freire is misled when he makes the teacher the culprit of educational wrongdoing, because students, too, must take responsibility for allowing this situation to continue in their classrooms.

It occurs to me now (very upsettingly, I might add), that in writing this paper that railed against Freire and Dr. Farmer, that I may have validated Freire in a way that I had not intended at the time. I had become so intent on throwing Freire in Dr. Farmer's face that I ultimately achieved what Freire would have wanted. I did not simply take the information, learn it, accept it, and regurgitate it for Dr. Farmer. I absorbed it, twisted it, turned it, cursed it, and tried my hardest to use it against the one who had shown it to me. Now, after pointing out the fallacy of Dr. Farmer's assignment, I fully understand that, even though my paper may not have been the response he wanted, Dr. Farmer taught me Freire on levels that I did not understand at the time. He personalized Freire's ideas, made them real to me without my realizing it.

It played out in my favor in the most immediate sense, I suppose. I received a passing grade on the assignment, and succeeded in, well, if not defeating, then at least confusing someone I regarded as my intellectual superior. And honestly, there were no sanctions that Dr. Farmer could impose on me in retaliation for my paper, even though what I said most certainly bordered on character assassination. You cannot preach educational freedom and then penalize someone for using it! (I remember feeling very smug when I wrote the last line of the paper, thinking to myself, "You can give me boundaries, but I'm going to do everything I can to mess up what's inside them.")

After three years, my initial defiance toward Freire and Dr. Farmer has led to a deeper understanding of what was trying to be said during those class sessions where I mounted my soapbox in vehement rebuttal. Educational freedom is a difficult subject to define, especially if you take into consideration the fact that all teachers teach from *some* bias. But that's another problem for another time. . . .

I would like to personally thank Dr. Farmer for allowing me to participate in this exchange. I think it's only fair to end this paper by making this point: I believe every word I said.

3 VOICE REPRISED
Three Etudes *for a Dialogic Understanding*

When I look back on my exchange with Devlyn, what occurs to me now are the many Bakhtinian ways that our dialogue could have been understood. As readers of the previous chapter know, I originally tried to explain Devlyn's writings through the frame of Aesopianism, through strategies for writing that managed to say something but, at the same time, evaded teacherly and institutional sanctions. After I received his closing response, however, I began to see that Devlyn's struggles with Freire—and my teaching of Freire—had much to do with Devlyn's attempt to negotiate what Bakhtin calls "internally persuasive" and "authoritative discourses." The latter, for Devlyn at least, was constituted of the words of his teacher, classmates, and Paulo Freire—words whose authority Devlyn was inspired to challenge. Thus, when Devlyn somewhat begrudgingly admits that he "did not simply take the information, learn it, accept it, and regurgitate it" but that rather he "absorbed it, twisted it, turned it, cursed it, and tried my hardest to use it against the one who had shown it to me," it would be hard to imagine a more concrete description of the process by which Bakhtin says one takes the alien word "and makes it one's own" (*DI* 294).

Yet there is another way to interpret Devlyn's struggle, one that highlights a key term in the Bakhtinian lexicon: *voice*. Now, it would be difficult for this reader of his work to characterize Devlyn as a writer who has no voice and is in search of one. No, Devlyn's voice is distinctive, self-assured, provocative to classmates and teacher alike. In our traditional ways of thinking about voice, we might be tempted to say that Devlyn's voice is a complete and sincere expression of his truest self—his values, beliefs, opinions, thoughts, and feelings, the tone of his very being. But to interpret Devlyn's voice this way is to ignore a number of questions to which Bakhtin would direct our attention: How can we think of Devlyn's voice as situated within a concert of voices? Whose voice (or voices) is Devlyn's in response to? Is Devlyn's voice in the process of becoming, changing? Can other voices be heard within the single voice we ascribe to Devlyn?

To ask these questions is to hint that our received understandings of voice may be inadequate, that something may, indeed, be happening to our traditional understandings of voice.

If I am right, voice is undergoing a kind of belated tent meeting, a high-spirited revival marked not by adulation for the featured soloist, but by appreciation for the chorus that makes the soloist possible, that which enables the soloist to sing and to be heard at all. This renewed interest in voice thus emerges out of the efforts of those scholars intent on rethinking voice from social and cultural perspectives. And such efforts, in all their variety, betoken an important departure from our received understandings of what we mean by voice in relation to the written word.[1]

Anne M. Greenhalgh, for example, explores the importance of voice in the context of teacher response to student drafts. Calling for a postmodern understanding of voice, Greenhalgh asks that we think of *"voices* in response" as indices not of personal but of social identities (304). This same call is heard from Linda Brodkey and James Henry, who, like Greenhalgh, find much promise in the ability to recognize how poststructural voice analysis is able to reveal the "subtle shifts in social identities that writers make in their texts" (155). As in Greenhalgh, Brodkey and Henry make use of the distinction between interruptive and interpretive voices, a distinction introduced by the British language analysts David Silverman and Brian Torode, to chart the ways that voices, in utterance and response, articulate social positionings. Important for teachers, Brodkey and Henry note, is that the modulation of any single voice "in the cycle of drafting, responding, and revising" can lead to generative shifts in all those other voices that express the many subject positions located "on either side of the desk" (155). More recently, two notable anthologies confirm our enduring interest in voice as a pedagogical concern. Peter Elbow's *Landmark*

Essays on Voice and Writing chronicles a number of important statements on the relationship of voice to writing, including some noteworthy contributions by the editor himself. Kathleen Blake Yancey's *Voices on Voice: Perspectives, Definitions, Inquiry* includes several new looks at problems related to voice, especially as these have recently been formulated along gender, ethnic, and cultural lines.

Closer to my purposes, though, are recent attempts to understand voice from a specifically dialogic perspective. Nancy Welch uses Bakhtin's notion of multivoicedness to expose the false dichotomies of form and content, of public and personal discourses, in student writing. In particular, Welch is interested in the kinds of responses to student writing that "promote conversation rather than allegiance," that listen for and engage those submerged voices between which an ongoing, creative dialogue might be sustained in future revisions (500-501).

Similarly, Joy Ritchie explores the writing workshop as an important locus for the intersection and struggle of competing voices, many of which require a degree of creative negotiation on the part of the individual student writer. The pedagogical benefits to be had from this struggle are likewise affirmed by Don H. Bialostosky, who sees voice not so much as the expression of a prior self, but rather as a relationship to all those other voices that constitute the self in its long journey toward what Bakhtin calls "ideological becoming" (Bialostosty, "Liberal" 13).

What all of these commentators share, in fact, is an awareness that voice is inescapably bound to the problem of selfhood, regardless of whether we choose to describe the self as a "subject position" or a "social identity" or a "dialogic intersection." All sense correctly, I believe, that what voice is able to express or represent is not a finished entity but an unfinished project, not an essence but a process, whose origins reside in particular social moments, institutions, and dialogues.

Here, I will elaborate what is sometimes only suggested by the authors noted above. That is, by examining voice in its *developmental*, *rhetorical*, and *historical* aspects, I offer three studies for how voice and its relationship to the self can be rethought from a dialogic perspective. To these ends, I draw extensively on the primary works of Mikhail Bakhtin and Lev Vygotsky, elaborating their complementary views on the problem of voice.[2] I conclude with some pedagogical strategies for incorporating a dialogic approach to voice in the writing classroom.

VOICE IN A DEVELOPMENTAL SENSE

For Vygotsky, voice is thoroughly implicated in the development of human consciousness. If we allow that the internalization of speech is, more precisely, the internalization of social *dialogue*, then it follows that what is internalized are the many voices encountered in the course of development. Further, if inner speech is the repository for internalized voices and if the central function of inner speech is verbal thought, then voice is necessary to human thinking. In other words, and as noted by many, we think *inside* those voices we have made our own.

The site for the most important voices we encounter is Vygotsky's now familiar zone of proximal development: "the distance between the actual developmental level as determined by independent problem solving and the level of potential development as determined through problem solving under adult guidance or in collaboration with more independent peers" (*Mind* 86). One logical implication of this idea is that the ability to solve problems through dialogue with more experienced adults or peers is a harbinger of competencies that will later become internalized. Vygotsky is thus interested in how the child, when confronted with a problem beyond her present capabilities, seeks help, asks questions, and responds to assistance in order to find a solution to that problem. These social interactions—interactions mediated by dialogue—are internalized and eventually "become part of the child's independent developmental achievement" (90).

Not surprisingly, then, Vygotsky holds that "the acquisition of language can serve as a paradigm for the entire problem of the relationship between learning and development" (89). Speech is capable of being learned only in and through social interactions, which is to say, within the ever-advancing borders of the zone of proximal development. In the long, slow process of acquiring the speech of others for her own purposes, the child transforms language's social, communicative function into an internal function that serves "to organize the child's thought" (89). That function, of course, is inner speech, a phenomenon resonating with the voices of all the heard others negotiated in social experience. Though Vygotsky himself made only passing allusions to the quality of voice, it is clear that his ideas regarding the nature of inner speech have been interpreted largely in vocal terms (see Kozulin 179; Ritchie 154; Trimbur 217; Wertsch' *Voices*). The writerly task of finding a voice, then, is inextricably linked to the developmental task of making a self, since the latter is ultimately an orchestration of the voices that inhabit itself. Yet common as such an expression may be, it is somewhat misleading to speak of "finding" a voice. To "find one's voice" is to suggest that voice is something uniform and static, a quality awaiting to be discovered by the one—the only one—to whom it properly belongs.

Vygotsky accurately surmises that this idealistic conception of selfhood—what he calls "the metaphysical theory of personality"—poses a considerable threat to his own "genetic" (developmental) conception of selfhood (*Thought* 67). There are several reasons for this, but primary among them is that, in essentialist conceptions of self, language is rendered superfluous, unnecessary to the development of the child. The "metaphysical personality," in other words, might use language to express the permanent features of its essential nature, but language *per se* has little to do with the developmental formation of that personality. Extrapolating from this observation, we would have to allow that voice likewise would be a thoroughly asocial phenomenon, having no need of other voices for its genesis. "True self" conceptions of voice, in other words, would discount, if not altogether exclude, the role language plays in the intellectual development of the human being. For all their praise of voice, those who champion a rhetoric of expression tend to overlook the crucial roles that *other voices* play in constructing that self presumably in quest of its own voice.[3]

Bakhtin shares with Vygotsky the basic idea that voices are originally social and thus necessarily appropriated from those around us. Bakhtin also holds that this appropriation is essential to the development of consciousness, noting that "everything that pertains to me enters my consciousness . . . from the external world through the mouths of others" (*SG* 138). Yet Bakhtin chooses a different word—

assimilation—to describe what is apparently the same process that Vygotsky refers to as internalization. The question occurs whether Vygotsky and Bakhtin do indeed refer to the same process—or more importantly, if they understand the same process in the same way. In response to the latter question at least, the answer is no.[4]

What Bakhtin contributes to the Vygotskian notion of internalization is the idea of a requisite *struggle*—the challenge that ensues in the difficult process of appropriating someone else's words for one's own purposes and the corresponding struggle among the interior voices that vie for ascendancy in consciousness. Apart from whatever other differences there may be between these terms, when Bakhtin uses *assimilation,* he does so believing that *struggle* is a basic feature of the process to which he refers. But why must the appropriation of other words, other voices, entail a struggle at all?

Bakhtin's answer to this question hinges upon his understanding of the nature of language itself. Bakhtin points out that "language is not a neutral medium that passes freely and easily into the private property of the speaker's intention" (*DI* 294). Instead, language exists in "a dialogically and tension-filled environment of alien words, value judgments, and accents" (276). Language, therefore, must be wrested from its previous "owners," so to speak. Thus, Bakhtin explains that "the word . . . exists in other people's mouths, in other people's contexts, serving other people's intentions: it is from there that one must take the word, and make it one's own" (294). The ensuing struggle is one of prying the word free from its myriad and erstwhile contexts. And yet, Bakhtin understands this process to be absolutely essential to the full realization of an individual consciousness.

Bakhtin's distinction between "authoritative discourse" and "internally persuasive discourse" illustrates something of the nature of this process. Authoritative discourse is "located in a distanced zone, organically connected with a past that is felt to be hierarchically higher. It is, so to speak, the word of the fathers. Its authority was already *acknowledged* in the past. It is a *prior discourse*" (342). Authoritative discourse, it may be said, is the received word, the word that does not allow any dialogizing challenge. By contrast, what Bakhtin calls internally persuasive discourse is discourse that ranges

freely among other discourses, that may be creatively recontextualized, and that is capable of engaging other discourses in dialogue. Its
importance to development, Bakhtin emphasizes, should not be
underestimated, since negotiating a consciousness of oneself, for oneself, is a long and complicated process of "distinguishing between
one's own and another's discourse, between one's own and another's
thought" (345).

Internally persuasive discourse, then, is "tightly interwoven with
'one's own word.'" It is "half-ours and half someone else's." Because
the internally persuasive word presupposes a measure of dialogue
with one's "own" words, along with other internally persuasive words,
it "does not remain in an isolated and static condition. It is not so
much interpreted by us," says Bakhtin, "as it is further, that is, freely
developed, applied to new material, new conditions; it enters into
interanimating relationships with new contexts" (345-46). What
accounts for the development of individual consciousness at all is
precisely the struggle that occurs between discourses, whether
authoritative or internally persuasive, a struggle that ultimately
enables us to reject those "discourses that do not matter to us, that do
not touch us" (345). As Bakhtin explains,

> The importance of struggling with another's discourse, its influence in
> the history of an individual's coming to ideological consciousness, is
> enormous. One's own discourse and one's own voice, although born of
> another or dynamically stimulated by another, will sooner or later
> begin to liberate themselves from the authority of another's discourse.
> This process is made more complex by the fact that a variety of alien
> voices enter into the struggle for influence within an individual's con-
> sciousness (just as they struggle with one another in surrounding social
> reality). (348)

Yes, Bakhtin might say, we *are* the voices that inhabit us, that
resound in our inner speech. But we are much more, since these
other voices do not merely coexist, indifferent to and estranged from
one another. Instead, a continuous rivalry takes place, a contest "for
hegemony among various available verbal and ideological points of
view, approaches, directions, and values" (346). Gary Saul Morson

and Caryl Emerson observe that, for Bakhtin, "selfhood is not a particular voice within, but a particular way of combining many voices within. Consciousness takes shape and never stops taking shape, as a process of interaction among authoritative and innerly persuasive discourses" (221).

What Bakhtin brings to the notion of internalized voices, then, is the idea of a necessary striving with the voices we have internalized or assimilated from others—many of which we find compatible with our situated purposes, many of which we do not. The important point is that at any given moment, the voice we choose to call our own is made possible by all those other voices which vie for hegemony in our consciousness, which form the chorus of voices against which our own may eventually be heard. It follows, then, that what we call consciousness is dialogic through and through, that the self is an event of language experience, and that neither consciousness nor emergent selfhood is able to attain the kind of crowning moment after which it may be said that this or that person is developmentally *finished.* Nothing could be further from the ideas of either Bakhtin or Vygotsky than to posit a developmental end-point, a coronation ritual to honor those who have, at long last, arrived.

VOICE IN A RHETORICAL SENSE

Apart from the many voices internalized or assimilated in inner speech, what of the many voices *encountered* in external, social speech? In other words, to what extent is voice a rhetorical construct, as well as a linguistic, psychological, or—as in the case of essentialist theories—a metaphysical one? Voice, in the understanding offered here, is rhetorical by virtue of its function of addressing or answering other voices—not only those voices encountered in our interpersonal relationships, but those that define the communities and cultures to which we belong.

From a Vygotskian perspective, voice is rhetorical because its manifestations in the zone of proximal development mark it as necessary to the meeting of desires and intentions within situations always involving others. Can there be any doubt that the voices that inhabit zones of proximal development are decidedly, and originally, rhetorical ones:

voices that ask for something *from* another, voices that ask something *of* another; voices that beseech and inquire, voices that guide and explore; voices that intend certain effects, voices that effect certain intentions? One feature of Vygotsky's theory seldom mentioned is that social speech, especially as it occurs within the zone of proximal development, is *rhetorical* speech. It is not supplanted by the development of inner or written speech, nor does it vanish on its own once other speech forms develop. To state the obvious, social speech remains a constant and necessary staple of human existence. For that reason, voice, in a rhetorical sense, is realized only in its relationship to, and difference from, other voices that it must address and answer. The quality of voice, in some measure, always presupposes other voices.

Bakhtin provides a fuller understanding of this point. Though he grants the reality of single-voiced discourse, Bakhtin is repelled by the desire for a single voice, equating such with a wish to take refuge from the demands of life itself: "A single voice ends nothing and resolves nothing. Two voices is the minimum for life, the minimum for existence" (*PDP* 252). Ultimately, one might say that single-voiced discourse *is* voiceless, since it is impossible to recognize a voice in isolation, that is, without the dialogizing background of those other voices against which it may be heard. The discernment of any particular voice, in fact, is accomplished by hearing it situated among all those *other* voices which it may mimic, ignore, or reject, with which it may agree or quarrel, from which it may borrow, and so on. This happens not merely because of the aural contrast provided by other voices. It happens because the voices against which any particular voice may be heard are voices that exist in *relationship* to that voice. Single-voiced discourse, in effect, precludes such relationship, refuses dialogue, since it neither answers nor addresses any other voice—nor does it feel any apparent need to. It is decidedly *arhetorical* in its orientation, imagining itself to be wholly sufficient to whatever task is at hand—a tale, a problem, a character, a truth, and so on. It needs no *other*.

Of course, such discourse holds little interest for Bakhtin, who prefers instead to conceive voice as something of a doubled phenomenon, both answering and anticipating an answer in every utterance. Because the voice that speaks the word is thoroughly implicated in the exigencies of *answering* and *addressing* the word of another, it can never be purely self-expressive, unaware or indifferent to another's word. It may aspire to this condition, as evidenced in Romantic aesthetics, but apart from "the mythical Adam" (*SG* 93), no one has since voiced an utterance wholly independent of the utterances of others. Bakhtin understands that all our efforts to persuade, convince, move, inform, affect, contend, agree—all our *rhetorical* efforts to influence one another are dialogically situated. The intentions we "author" in everyday discourse are simultaneously active and responsive, original and derivative, initiated and received. All our efforts to influence someone through *address* are simultaneously attempts to *answer someone else*—at the very least, that same someone whose answer we anticipate and build into our addressing utterance. No one speaks in a vacuum; no voice is heard apart from those voices it answers and addresses. Dialogue, in other words, needs its "other words."

Like Vygotsky, Bakhtin posits an essentially rhetorical dimension to the quality of voice, and also like Vygotsky, he understands this dimension to be contingent on the process of dialogue, in particular, on the basic features of answerability and addressivity. Unlike his contemporary, though, Bakhtin understands these features to be simultaneously present in the structure of each and every utterance, which is why voice is always *voices*. A voice in isolation has no reason to speak, no motive to be heard, and thus is meaningless.

VOICE IN A HISTORICAL SENSE

There remains, however, a final sense in which voice may be said to be social, and that sense we could call the *historical*. As one committed to a Marxist psychology, Vygotsky was interested in questions regarding how sociocultural knowledge is transmitted within the contexts of historical milieus and constraints—how, in other words, a given culture in a given historical moment becomes a part of the consciousness of its individual members. Vygotsky thus posits "the internalization of socially rooted and historically developed activities [as] the distinguishing feature of human psychology" (*Mind* 57). And, of course, that internalization is accomplished through the mediating and transformative power of signs, the most profound of which is speech, or as I argue here, the dialogue of voices occurring in the developmental history of the individual.

Now the voices that become internalized are not abstractions. They carry with them all "the musical, expressive, intonational qualities" that oral speech is capable of manifesting (*Thought* 181). Indeed, it is precisely these qualities that account for some measure of the "shared apperception" that occurs between interlocutors in social dialogue, the understanding that results from the fact that "each person can see his partners, their facial expressions and gestures, and *hear the tone of their voices*" (my emphasis, 240). Vygotsky borrows a passage from Dostoevsky to illustrate the kind of extreme abbreviation possible when such nonverbal clues lend meaning to a specific utterance— or, as in Dostoevsky's excerpt, a specific word.[5] Referring to that passage, Vygotsky notes how a change of voice signifies a change in meaning:

> Here we see one more source of the abbreviation of oral speech, i.e., the modulation of voice that reveals psychological context within which a word is to be understood. In Dostoevsky's story it was contemptuous negation in one case, doubt in another, anger in the third. We have discovered so far two factors of abbreviation. One is connected with shared apperception by the persons involved in dialogue; the other occurs *when the idea can be rendered by inflection.* (emphasis added, 242)

In dialogue, understanding is often a function of the contexts revealed through, or invoked by, the uttering voice. Misunderstanding, then, often results from the fact that words have potential meanings, a multitude of contexts in which they may be spoken and heard (and thus misspoken and misheard). Vygotsky refers to this context-dependency of signification as a word's *sense*, which he contrasts with a word's *meaning:*

> the sense of a word . . . is the sum of all the psychological events aroused in our consciousness by the word. It is a dynamic, fluid, complex whole, which has several zones of unequal stability. Meaning is only one of the zones of sense, the most stable and precise zone. A word acquires its sense from the context in which it appears; in different contexts, it changes its sense. The dictionary meaning of a word is no more than a stone in the

edifice of sense, no more than a potentiality that finds diversified realization in speech. (244-45)

Vygotsky observes that, in inner speech, sense predominates over meaning and is, in great measure, the very content of inner speech. Because a word's sense is dependent on the contexts in which it is voiced and because sense constitutes the larger portion of inner speech, it is reasonable to infer that *the various contexts of oral speech are amenable to internalization.* Stated a bit differently, we do not internalize words removed from the situated voices that speak them. Rather, when we receive words through the utterances of others, we internalize a repertoire of potential contexts in which those same words may be heard and understood. Though Vygotsky does not elaborate the specific role of voice in sociocultural understanding, his writings clearly imply that voice is one important conduit for the historical formation of mind.

Bakhtin more pointedly argues that voices possess the ability to suggest, echo, resonate the varied and prior contexts in which they have been heard. For Bakhtin, voice is historical because it is able to recall those places where it has been spoken. It carries with it the accumulated tones and overtones, accents and traces, sounds and shadings of all its journeys. As Bakhtin puts it, "each word tastes of the context or contexts in which it has lived its socially charged life." (*DI* 293).

Bakhtin and Vygotsky share a recognition that meaning is dependent on social and historical contexts. From Bakhtin's point of view, context is why the utterance is an unrepeatable phenomenon, why we hear not signs but tones, why utterances assume those sociohistorical forms known as speech genres. Every dictionary "meaning" thus is inadequate to the task that it undertakes since no word is "uninhabited by others' voices. . . . The word enters his [the speaker's] context from another context, permeated with the interpretations of others" (*PDP* 202).

Bakhtin often chooses to make this point in less personal, more cultural terms. "All words," according to Bakhtin, "have the 'taste' of a profession, a genre, a tendency, a party, a particular work" (*DI* 293).

In fact, this tension between the personal and the sociohistorical is something of a constant in Bakhtin's thought. Two things that Bakhtin mentions in this regard—tonality and genre—speak directly to that tension, since tonality implies the personal, individual qualities of expression, while genre more readily suggests those historical forms that surpass personality, uniqueness. Indeed, Bakhtin adds considerable sophistication to our present understanding of voice by demonstrating how genres "lend" expressive tonality to the individual, situationally-bound voice.

When we make an utterance, Bakhtin notes, we take words "from other utterances, and mainly from utterances that are kindred to ours in genre" (*SG* 87). The words we "borrow" are not gleaned from dictionaries, but from those social forms of utterances known as speech genres, received forms of concrete, practical usage. Our speech, then, is largely, and necessarily, generic. This is not to say that any particular speaker's utterance is devoid of individual accents, overtones, or peculiarities. But such qualities are, in some measure, bequeathed to us. Genres, that is, are a *copia* of tonalities; "their structure," Bakhtin adds, "includes a certain expressive intonation" (79). In fact, Bakhtin holds that our ability to express our personal individuality *within* genres proceeds from the degree of mastery we have *of* genres, of their range and diversity. The more accomplished our command of the genres of everyday speech, "the more freely we employ them, the more fully and clearly we reveal our own individuality in them" (80).

Obviously, we are in the midst of paradox here. Bakhtin claims that what best allows individualized expression is a mastery of speech genres, that what accounts for the "unrepeatable situation of communication" is our command of the generic forms into which any given utterance may be cast. Even a quality so obviously personal as "tone of voice" can be understood as social if, first, we recognize that the speaking person is constituted of the many voices (and genres that organize those voices) negotiated throughout social experience and, second, that the desirable quality of "having a voice" may be a function of having a wide familiarity with the abundant, highly-differentiated speech genres into which our individual utterances are cast. Morson and Emerson thus hold that "as our psychic life grows more and more complex, we develop new ways to reaccentuate the discourse of others. In this respect, too, the self, as an assimilator of discourses, resembles a novel" (220).

Indeed, we are forever representing other discourses, other genres, other voices within our own speech. As this happens, we reaccentuate those other voices by virtue of the fact that we locate ourselves in relation to them. We cannot escape the necessity of having to evaluate the words of others for the very reason that our own speech is "full of other people's words." But, Bakhtin argues, "with some of them we completely merge our own voice, forgetting whose they are; others, which we take as authoritative, we use to reinforce our own words; still others, finally, we populate with our own aspirations, alien or hostile to them" (*PDP* 195). One might say, then, we novelize our speech to the extent that we incorporate other people's words into those we typically regard to be our own. But exactly how can we tell the difference between our words and someone else's?

The answer to this question, again, hinges on how we conceive ourselves. Should we come to understand the self as more a process than an entity, as an orchestration of the many voices inhabiting our consciousness, we cannot escape the conclusion that at any given moment we have incomplete access to who we are or who we claim to be. Thus, what we call our own voice is not likely to be identical to our prior and future assessments of that "same" voice. To get a sense of how this is so, Morson and Emerson suggest that each of us need only peruse our own collected writings. Who has not discovered that

> it is painful to encounter . . . an old letter, old notes, a diary entry, something that brings to mind an intense inner argument—of how one used to orchestrate inner dialogues, because we recognize how large a role was played by voices and perspectives that we have since rejected or outgrown in ourselves and criticize in others. Writers may reject old works that are in fact quite successful because the inner voices informing them now seem alien, threatening, or in danger of reasserting themselves. (*Prosaics*, 222)

They go on to add that one could "understand a great deal about the development of a writer" if one could study "the complex process of assimilation and reaccentuation of inner voices" (222-23). What they conclude is that our intellectual growth in general and our growth as writers in particular are both shaped through the relationships with the voices we engage in dialogue.

IMPLICATIONS FOR THE WRITING CLASSROOM

At the outset, I suggested that a dialogic understanding of voice required a dialogic understanding of selfhood. Don H. Bialostosky has observed that the dialogic self is "created in the course of . . . assimilating, responding to, and anticipating the voices of others" ("Liberal," 13). Thus, and as I have tried to show here, voice is always a *relationship* to other voices, including (and especially) those that go into the formation of our uttering selves. Any dialogic approach to voice, then, will emphasize the relational, plural quality that voice entails. Given this starting point, what can we infer from the theories of Vygotsky and Bakhtin that might have practical applications for the writing classroom? How might a uniquely dialogic approach to voice manifest itself in the pedagogies we devise for our students?

First, and from a developmental perspective, I would argue that we need to broaden our understanding of the zone of proximal development to include a textual, or intertextual, dimension. Vygotsky's research, of course, was designed to understand the process of concept formation in early childhood development, and subsequent research along these lines, especially on the acquisition of voice, has likewise focused on subjects of a very young age.[6] Yet if development is, in fact, ongoing and unceasing, then we must allow that the zone of proximal development has a place in advanced writing instruction as well. Obviously, the teacher-student conference most closely approximates the dyadic exchanges that characterize the methods of Vygotsky and later researchers. But, as writing teachers, we are obliged to affirm that when our students confront written voices different from their own, the opportunity exists for students to learn from those other voices, even when such voices are textually inscribed.

Texts, of course, instruct in explicit, often didactic ways, but that is not at all what I have in mind. A dialogic understanding of textuality, rather, would hear texts as utterances able to "smuggle in" the implied argument of competing perspectives and to convey these perspectives through the many voices which texts are able to orchestrate. Our students' encounter with unfamiliar voices, then, carries with it the possibility for engaging such voices in ways analogous to the dialogues that occur between parent and child, teacher and student, peer and advanced peer—all the forms usually associated with the zone of proximal development. In this way, the uttering text becomes something of a vicarious interlocutor, challenging the student with a different worldview or a previously unheard voice and, quite possibly, the rhetorical occasion for a needed response.

The recent trend in composition textbooks to include voices traditionally excluded or marginalized is laudable in this respect, but only so long as such unfamiliar voices are not merely appreciated but engaged, not merely heard but answered. Here, Bakhtin's anticipation of a requisite struggle comes into play, for the simple juxtaposition of multiple voices is relatively unimportant to development. What's crucial to the nurturance of a dialogic consciousness, rather, is the interanimation of voices in dialogue and the formidable difficulties involved in making those voices our own, of making them internally persuasive and thus able to be "freely developed, applied to new material, new conditions . . . new contexts" (*DI* 345).

Two activities, then, are suggested by these ideas. First is the need to *answer* the myriad and (initially) alien voices we might choose to introduce to our students. Dialogue journals can be (and have been) used successfully for this purpose; but the same benefits can be found in the need to respond to the voices that inhabit quoted sources and thus demarcate the rich territory between reporting and reported discourses. The authorial need to frame reported discourses cannot help but to situate the author in a *responsive* position to whatever sources he or she calls upon. Constructing assignments that ask students to deploy, and stake a position in relation to, other voices from their readings (especially those other voices that embody competing perspectives) is asking students to become participants in a dialogue, to give voice to their own perspectives on the question at hand.

But the second activity suggested by a dialogic understanding is the need to *revoice* those other voices, to recontextualize those voices for purposes distinct from the ones for which they might have been originally intended. Much like the novelist, students should also possess the opportunity to ventriloquize those other voices in ways that necessitate, as Bakhtin says, "having to choose a language" (*DI* 295). Elsewhere, I have tried to demonstrate how this might occur in a writing unit that explores the neurological condition known as prosopagnosia. Leading students through definitions gleaned from medical dictionaries, followed by Oliver Sacks's "The Man Who Mistook His Wife For A Hat," followed, in turn, by "Review of Research on Prosopagnosia" by Antonio Damasio, I intentionally confront students with myriad perspectives—thus myriad voices— on the same condition. Students learn much about a rare pathology, of course, but they also learn that the same condition can be known in different ways, in different languages, through different voices.

The final assignment for this unit, in fact, asks students to explain prosopagnosia to next year's class who, likewise, will know nothing about this unusual disease. Thus, not only do students acquire a sense of themselves as developing knowers, but their sense of audience awareness depends precisely on the ability to remember their prior concerns and apprehensions when the unit began. More important, students are confronted with the problem of how best to explain their newly acquired knowledge to uninformed peers. Faced with the rhetorical exigency of "having to choose a language" for the purpose of explaining *this subject, given this situation,* students not only must appropriate the voices of experts on this topic, but must choose an expert voice of their own by which to orchestrate all those *other voices* to establish an authorial position among them. Conditions for the kind of generative struggle to which Bakhtin refers are thus cultivated by design, and the novice-expert relationships that typify Vygotsky's zone of proximal development are shown to be transitional: novices can and do become experts, and such newly-acquired expertise can be textually voiced.

In teaching voice from a *rhetorical* perspective, we might do well to stress the many ways that texts *answer* one another and (correspondingly) anticipate how they themselves will be answered. Despite the convention of thematic groupings, our anthologies do not always

encourage tracing the lineage of intertextual conversations, often pre-
ferring instead a "great essays" approach, which offers monuments of
fine writing whose self-evident virtues apparently transcend dialogue. In any event, such a weakness can be turned to our advantage,
particularly if we ask students to fill in the missing links, as Bakhtin
would say, "in the chain of speech communion" (*SG* 84).

A frequently anthologized piece, for example, like Martin Luther
King's "Letter From a Birmingham Jail," can be the occasion for having students reconstruct what those Birmingham clergymen must
have said in order to provoke King's eloquent rejoinder. In keeping
with the corporate authorship of the original utterance, students are
placed in small groups and asked to draft a version of the document
to which King responded. To accomplish this task, students must pay
close attention not only to what King says, but also to what he implies
that his interlocutors have said. Moreover, students are asked to consider if King's chosen "tone of voice" could have any rhetorical significance for his audience and, in fact, whether King might not be
speaking to an audience larger than a group of local clergy.

Of course, students express a great deal of curiosity regarding how
closely each group's response "matched up" with the original; but
there is abundant interest, as well, in how each group approached this
task and the reasons each group gave as to why *these* arguments are
presented in *this* order and in *that* voice. Further discussion centers
upon how and where King anticipated what might be said in response
to his letter and what, if anything, he did to preempt unwanted
responses. Additionally, students are asked to identify where King
moves to keep open this dialogue, to identify passages composed to
keep this dialogue open, to steer it in directions [that] King thinks
might be more productive.

A useful follow-up assignment is to have students write another
group response to King's letter—this time in their own voices, as students writing some thirty years after King wrote his famous letter.
Does King have anything to say to address the racial problems
America faces today? Are his solutions relevant, his ideas enduring?
Does he speak to the pertinent issues? Or more tellingly perhaps, does
he speak in voices that resonates among young Americans, especially

young African-Americans? Explorations of this sort go far in rein-
forcing the notion that texts are situated instances of address and
rejoinder, utterances that seek to be heard, understood, answered—
even across years, decades, centuries, within the expanse of what
Bakhtin calls "great time" (*SG* 4).

Such explorations also go far in revealing how voices emerge in
historical and social contexts, how one voice is capable of recontextu-
alizing a number of historical voices for contemporary purposes.
King's appropriation of Old Testament phrasing and cadence, when
reaccentuated in African-American idioms, spoke powerfully to a
generation ready to hear a voice of moral authority, a voice able to
speak compellingly to a plurality of distinct traditions. Less urgently
perhaps, but no less powerfully, the appropriation of historical voices
by writers working in different genres has likewise been put to good
effect. Though his understanding of voice is different from the one I
offer here, Peter Elbow has argued that a characteristic quality of
Richard Selzer's voice is his sonorous orchestration of Shakespearean
and biblical languages—both appropriated for contexts that neither
could foresee, yet both echoing occasions where they had once been
declaimed, namely, "the stage and the pulpit" ("Pleasures," 213).

Such examples, along with Bakhtin's explication of double-voicing
in a brief passage from *Little Dorrit,* suggest that there may be considerable value in teaching our students to listen for the diverse voices at
large in the texts we ask them to read. For without the ability to hear
other voices, our students' faith in the possibility for writing in and
through those voices, of making such voices their own, will be a
diminished one. Importantly, though, the analysis of textual voices I
advocate here must not separate voices from the contexts in which
they are heard and which they themselves are able to suggest or recall.
The tempting alternative—to study voices in isolation, with an eye
toward identifying the empirical features of a single voice—is contrary to the understanding of voice offered by Vygotsky and Bakhtin.
Voice lessons are necessarily history lessons, too.

Finally, then, what do we tell that student earnestly seeking her true
voice? Obviously, from what's been said here, the notion of one "true
voice" is more than a little suspect. We might do well by this student if

we encourage her, instead, to consider finding her true voices. In challenging her received ideas of voice as a permanent feature of an essential self, we also challenge the limitations, rhetorical and otherwise, that a single voice entails. We might point out to her that when we say of ourselves or a peer or a favorite author that he or she has a *voice,* we have done little more than remove that voice from all those other voices it seeks to answer and address. We might point out that every writer has a chorus of voices—some advancing, some receding; some appropriate, some misplaced; some preferred, some resisted. Our task—a difficult one, to be sure—is to deliver voice from its long romance with the true self and return it to the arena of living dialogue from whence it derives its only meaning: the colloquy of other voices.

If we do this, we might even relieve our imaginary student of the burden of thinking she must possess a single, unchanging voice that is hers alone—and the silence that eventually occurs when she, and her classmates, realize this burden is impossible to meet.

4 SOUNDING THE OTHER WHO SPEAKS IN ME
Toward a Dialogic Understanding of Imitation

> What is wanted . . . is a fundamental intersecting of
> languages in a single given consciousness, one that
> participates equally in several languages.
>
> *M. M. Bakhtin*

Among present-day compositionists, there seems to be little doubt that imitation has all but disappeared from serious consideration as a viable practice in writing instruction. Edward Corbett's claim that imitation has little chance of making a "comeback" seems as prescient now as it did when it was first made some thirty years ago (249). Indeed, it has been eloquently reiterated by Robert Connors, who, in a recent essay on the erasure of sentence rhetorics, sees imitation's demise as the result of our discipline's wholesale rejection of formalism, behaviorism, and empiricism in favor of attitudes toward texts more agreeable to English departments than to departments of speech, psychology, or education—the supposed originators of our prior fascination with the sentence (120-21). Regardless, for many teachers of writing, imitation has been so thoroughly discredited that it may now be looked upon as something of a quaint vestige of days gone by, an amusing holdover from far more benighted times than our own.

Yet there are formidable stumbling blocks that must be overcome in our attempts to eulogize imitation as a pedagogical practice. One of the more baffling difficulties to be met is that despite imitation's reported demise, there exists an abundant literature on its value to the writing classroom. From the very beginnings of the process movement, a fairly large number of scholars in rhetoric and composition have vigorously championed the usefulness of imitation in the teaching of writing. Indeed, a remarkably varied and rich literature on imitation emerged during a time when imitation's fortunes were, in the view of Corbett and many other informed observers, on the decline.[1]

How, then, to explain this paradox? A few years ago, Phillip Arrington and I conducted an extensive review of the ample literature on imitation. Our purpose was to give an account of imitation's vexed status within our discipline; our method was to regard the many articles, chapters, papers about imitation as utterances situated within a dialogic context. What we found is that, apart from how pedagogically specific any individual article (utterance) might be, the characteristic feature of nearly all writing about imitation was the need to *justify* its usage. We grouped all such justifications into what we thought were the four most likely and predominant categories: stylistic, inventional, interventional, and social. We then argued that the ubiquitous, overwhelming need to justify imitation was, in some considerable measure, evidence that imitation had been *tacitly* rejected by our community at large and that those who championed imitation knew this to be the case. Otherwise, we reasoned, the literature on imitation would not be so abundant; its proponents would be more centrally concerned with refinements for its use; and critics of imitation would feel the need to be explicit in their opposition. We thus concluded that, indeed, imitation was a largely discredited practice among current writing teachers and scholars.

We nonetheless elected to close our review by hinting that maybe it was premature to sound imitation's death-knell, that perhaps there were other ways to think about imitation that had not been previously considered. In keeping with the dialogic approach we chose for our literature review, we suggested that it might be possible to think about imitation dialogically and indicated that two likely sources for such an endeavor could be found in the writings of Lev Vygotsky and Mikhail Bakhtin, especially the latter.

Of course, others before us had noticed that certain aspects of Bakhtin's work seemed to warrant a rethinking of imitation. In the one essay most responsible for introducing Bakhtin to compositionists, Charles Schuster had already pointed out that imitation, as a

pedagogical practice, becomes vastly more interesting and approach-
able when regarded from a Bakhtinian perspective:

> When we think of the kinds of accents and intonations that can enter into
> language from other speakers, heroes, listeners, and languages we begin to
> establish a perspective from which we can understand more sophisticated
> language use such as sarcasm, parody, and irony. We begin to see how style
> develops through the imitation of—and association with—other styles.
> (598)

But in a disciplinary milieu wherein questions pertaining to style
received scant attention at best, Schuster's passing observation about
imitation did not spark any particular interest in its rethinking.

Nor, for that matter, did the work of Jon Klancher. In "Bakhtin's
Rhetoric," Klancher took a decidedly ideological approach in trying
to determine what Bakhtin has to offer the writing classroom.
Klancher argues that both paraphrase and parody, from a Bakhtinian
view, are capable of suggesting a "pedagogy whose aim is to disengage
student writers from crippling subservience to the received languages
they grapple with" (89). Klancher proposes that writing assignments
ask students to parody the languages of others, so long as parody
entails "not the lesser exercise of imitation, but the frankly critical,
dialogically informed encounter between social languages" (93).
Klancher clearly hoped to draw a qualitative distinction between
those kinds of imitation (e.g., paraphrase, parody) that are "critical,
dialogically informed" and those, we are to assume, that constitute
the more traditional brands aligned with the "servile copying" and
"mindless aping" sorts of old.

More recently, Mary Minock has asked for a reconsideration of imitation in light of certain strands of postmodern theory, especially as
such strands come to us through the work of Jacques Derrida, Jacques
Lacan, and Mikhail Bakhtin. Of these thinkers, in fact, it is Bakhtin who
figures most prominently in Minock's argument. Reiterating Bakhtin's
point that, understood dialogically, the boundary line between one's
own words and another's words is always malleable, always elastic,
always permeable, Minock argues that the unconscious imitation of
another's words is crucial to the continuance of any dialogue with those

words. To maintain and to further dialogue, therefore, we must first know how to speak the words *of* another as a requisite for dialogue *with* the other (494-95). If I understand her correctly, Minock is not too far from the view that imitation, from a Bakhtinian perspective, is something of a condition of possibility for dialogue.

Along with Schuster, Klancher, and others, Minock points to the likelihood that Bakhtin's theory of dialogue ought, at the very least, to encourage us to take another look at imitation. In the following pages, I would like to do just that. More specifically, I would like to sketch out the features of what I call a dialogic imitation, illuminating, among other things, where and how a dialogic approach to imitation would differ from our received understandings of the term. Before offering a model for what I propose, however, it will be useful to review exactly what Bakhtin has to say about imitation.[2]

BAKHTIN AND IMITATION

On the face of things, we might expect Bakhtin to have absolutely no interest whatsoever in imitation. After all, it is hard to imagine a more *antidialogic* concept—literary, rhetorical, pedagogical, or otherwise— than that of imitation. Indeed, and as I suggested in the introduction to this work, silence itself might seem more potentially dialogic than the rote duplication of another's words, if only because parroted words, unlike certain silences, are addressed to no one. As if to emphasize this point, when Bakhtin chooses a counter term for dialogue, he does not offer silence but rather, monologue. And yet, insofar as language learning is concerned, it would seem that, for many, these terms ultimately become identical, since efforts directed toward imitating another's word, for most of us, could only be interpreted as a wish to merge with that word in some sort of monologic unity, that is to say, in undifferentiated silence.[3]

Ought we to conclude, then, that Bakhtin discusses imitation only for the purpose of illuminating the salient features of what he means by dialogue, of highlighting his privileged term, dialogue, by contrasting it with an opposite term that he disparages? No, this does not seem to be the probable motive for Bakhtin's scattered remarks on imitation. Rather, Bakhtin's comments on imitation emerge within the varied contexts of his working through larger problems and concerns. Thus, if we are to glean something of what Bakhtin thought about imitation, we must return to those contexts to understand what Bakhtin is saying about imitation and then explore whether or not it is possible to formulate a coherent understanding of how Bakhtin regarded imitation.

Imitation and Novelistic Discourse

It is within his varied discussions of the novel where we find Bakhtin evince an interest in the relationship of imitation to dialogue. Bakhtin is fully aware that the kind of novel he describes is very much situated in the *mimetic* tradition. The distinguishing feature in Bakhtin's understanding of the novel, however, is not the imitation of "reality" as such, nor the Aristotelian imitation of dramatic action, but instead the representation of the human voice, which is always and everywhere for Bakhtin, the imitation of the multiple voices that constitute social existence (Bialostosky, "Booth's").

Now, in light of the centrality of "the speaking person and his discourse" to Bakhtin's definition of the novel, it should come as no great surprise to hear Bakhtin aver that any stylistics of the novel must begin with the problem of *"artistically representing language, the problem of representing the image of a language"* (*DI* 336). One might point out that every mimetic conception of the novel has understood this to be a problem, whether explicitly acknowledged or no. But where Bakhtin complicates matters is in his realization that a represented language is always a *representing* language, that a represented language gives voice to *other voices*, that a represented language may even "talk back" to the author whose utterances presumably determine the whole of the novelistic discourse. The complexities of mapping out the dialogic relationships in any novelistic discourse are abundant and complex, as is obvious in Bakhtin's chart of discourses available to the novelist.

In *Problems of Dostoevsky's Poetics*, Bakhtin offers such a schematic of available discourse types. Among single-voiced discourses, for example, Bakhtin first identifies what he calls *direct, unmediated discourse*, a single-voiced discourse that simply has no need of another voice. It is discourse, as Bakhtin explains, "directed exclusively toward its referential object" by a speaker whose "ultimate semantic authority" is sufficient and absolute (99). David Lodge points out that this discourse type corresponds to Plato's description of *diegesis,* the representation of reality in the voice of the poet (or narrator) (33). A second kind of single-voiced discourse is *objectified discourse,* words that attempt to represent the speech of a character "objectively." This type corresponds to Plato's mimesis and would obviously include direct quotation, but also, as Lodge reminds, various types of reported speech (33). More to my purposes here, though, are the varieties of *double-voiced discourse*—or, as Bakhtin says, speech "with an orientation toward someone else's discourse" (*PDP* 199). Bakhtin identifies three main types.

First, there is a passive type of double-voiced discourse that Bakhtin calls *unidirectional double-voiced discourse.* It includes stylization, *skaz* (narrator's narration), "the unobjectified discourse of a character" for authorial intentions, and forms of first-person narration. What these share, according to Bakhtin, "is an intention on the part of the author to make use of someone else's discourse in the direction of its own particular aspirations" (*PDP* 193). While two voices are present, only one referential direction may be perceived, that of the author. As Morson and Emerson point out, in passive discourse, the author "uses the other's discourse for his own purposes, and if he allows it to be heard and sensed, that is because his purposes require it to be" (*Prosaics,* 150).

Vari-directional double-voiced discourse, too, is a passive type of double-voiced discourse, but one where the author's purposes are different from the purposes of the "hero" or "character" or generalized "other." This type is passive because, most often, the discourse of the other is at odds with the discourse of the author, who, in order to evaluate the other critically, parodies or ironizes his speech. The other is unwittingly at the mercy of the author; their purposes diverge, and the other is vulnerable to the author's subterfuge. Obviously, then, this type of discourse includes all forms of parody, including what Bakhtin calls "parodic skaz."

Finally, there is *active double-voiced discourse.* Here, Bakhtin observes, the discourse of the other resists the exclusive purposes of the author, enters into dialogue with the author's discourse, and is able to modify, persuade, affect the author's intentions. Bakhtin claims that in discourse of this type, "the other's words actively influence the author's speech, forcing it to alter itself accordingly" (*PDP* 197). This is the most authentically dialogic of all forms of double-voicing and is, for Bakhtin, best exemplified in the novels of Dostoevsky. Under this category, Bakhtin places such forms of discourse as "hidden polemic," "hidden dialogue," "rejoinder in a dialogue," the word with "a sideward glance," and certain forms of parody, so long as the parodied language "answers" the language of the parodist author.

Bakhtin is quick to point out that his schematic is at best extremely limited, since, as he admits, "we have far from exhausted all the possible examples of double-voiced discourse" (*PDP* 198). But the classification system above should offer some insight into the remarkably complex variations that occur not only within the novel itself, but also within the relationships that the novel establishes with other extant genres. We have already seen, for example, how parody figures prominently in the discourse that occurs between and among characters and authors within a novel. But the novel, as a genre, parodies other novels and other genres as well. One of the ways, for example, that the novel relativizes other genres is through its open contentiousness with those genres. As Bakhtin himself says of the novel: "throughout its entire history there is a consistent parodying or travestying of dominant or fashionable novels that attempt to become models for the genre" (*DI* 6).

Parody may also be heard in the novel's representation of those languages within a language that Bakhtin refers to as *heteroglossia*, where, for example, such carnivalized genres as "street songs, folk-sayings, anecdotes," and the "low" genres of laughter consciously parody the "official languages of [their] given time" (*DI* 273). It can also be witnessed in the myriad languages that accompany the realities of everyday life. Bakhtin asks us to consider an "illiterate peasant" who "prayed to God in one language . . . sang songs in another . . . spoke to his family in a third and . . . [petitioned] local authorities through a scribe" in yet a fourth (*DI* 296). So long as this peasant is able to compartmentalize these distinct languages, each will remain "indisputable," that is, the peasant will be unable "to regard one language (and the verbal world corresponding to it) through the eyes of another language" (*DI* 296-97). However, once the peasant experiences the "critical interanimation of languages" in his own consciousness, the nature of each is radically altered, the hegemony of each compromised, the authority of each eroded. What ensues, instead, is a dialogic awareness that no particular worldview is beyond challenge, that is to say, indisputable.

This newly acquired dialogic consciousness is precisely what the novel concerns itself with. The languages of heteroglossia that interanimate each other in an individual's consciousness find outward expression "on the plane of the novel," the one genre capable of adequately representing the stratification of languages in a given social milieu, as well as the dialogue that occurs between such languages. Moreover, once integrated into the novel, heteroglossia cannot help but be what Bakhtin calls "a special type of *double-voiced discourse*," since heteroglossia in the novel must necessarily represent "the direct intention of the character who is speaking, and the refracted intention of the author" (*DI* 324). As in all double-voiced discourse, "two voices, two meanings, and two expressions" may be discerned. Moreover, as Bakhtin suggests, the double-voicedness of heteroglossia is of the *active* sort, because the two voices involved "know about each other (just as two exchanges in a dialogue know of each other and are structured in this mutual knowledge of each other" (*DI* 324).

To demonstrate at least partially why this is so and, at the same time, to reveal something of how Bakhtin understood imitation, it will be useful to return to Bakhtin's observations on that particular type of double-voiced discourse that he calls stylization.

Recall that Bakhtin regards stylization to be a "unidirectional" type of passive double-voiced discourse. The stylizer, as Bakhtin says, "works with someone else's point of view," or perhaps more exactly, "with the other's speech as an expression of a particular point of view" (*PDP* 189). Because stylization is a double-voiced discourse, there can be no merging of author and character's voices or perspectives. For this reason, Bakhtin points out, stylized discourse is *conditional*, that is, the author, while retaining the style of the character speaking, has nonetheless penetrated that character's speech with his own attitude, his own voice. The "objectified" discourse of the character "now serves new purposes, which take possession of it from within" and remove from it the possibility of being a thoroughly "earnest" discourse, since the character's discourse must now accommodate the author's intentions (*PDP* 190). Bakhtin goes on to note that "conditional discourse is always double-voiced" and hints that the same discourse was once "unconditional, in earnest" (*PDP* 190).

Bakhtin's observations on the conditionality of double-voiced discourse are important for a number of reasons, one of which is to provide him with a criterion by which to distinguish stylization from imitation—imitation, that is, as traditionally (or narrowly) understood:

> Imitation does not render a form conditional, for it takes the imitated material seriously, makes it its own, directly appropriates to itself someone else's discourse. What happens in that case is a complete merging of voices, and if we do hear another's voice, then it is certainly not one that had figured into the author's plan. (*PDP* 190)

Bakhtin warns that the stylizer is susceptible to crossing over into imitation, "should the stylizer's enthusiasm for his model destroy the distance and weaken the deliberate sense of a reproduced style as *someone else's style*" (*PDP* 190). If and when that occurs, the possibility for dialogue vanishes, since author and character have become one, and dialogue, therefore, has become unnecessary. Essential, then, to stylization, to all forms of double-voiced discourse, and to all manifestations of dialogue is the clear perception of *someone else speaking*, the voice of a necessary other without whom dialogue is impossible.

These observations, as noted above, are made in the context of Bakhtin's discussion of the novel, in particular, the range of author-character ("hero") relationships available to novelistic discourse. As I will show later, it is possible to make certain inferences about imitation in writing pedagogy from Bakhtin's limited remarks on double-voiced discourse in the novel. But what, if anything, does Bakhtin have to say about the role of imitation in more prosaic contexts?

Imitation and Everyday Discourse

Given Bakhtin's understanding of the novel as outlined above, it should come as no great surprise that, for Bakhtin, no absolute division exists between novelistic and everyday discourses. Just as the novel is able to give free expression to the discourses of contemporary, everyday life, Bakhtin likewise seems to indicate that all of the forms of discourse available to the novelist are also available to the speaker of everyday discourse, that is, to oneself as the "author" of one's own utterance. In everyday discourse, Bakhtin argues, we constantly appropriate someone else's words for our own purposes; we constantly represent the speech of others. What determines our particular relationship to the languages we borrow are the "tasks" before us, the discursive intentions we wish to effect. Bakhtin elaborates upon this notion of the speaker as author:

> During everyday verbal transmission of another's words, the entire complex of discourse . . . may be expressed and even played with (in the form of an exact replication to a parodic ridiculing and exaggeration of gestures and intonations). This representation is always subordinated to the tasks of practical, engaged transmission and is wholly determined by these tasks. This of course does not involve the artistic image of his discourse, and even less the image of a language. Nevertheless, everyday episodes involving the same person, when they become linked, already entail prose devices for the double-voiced and even double languaged representation of another's words. (*DI* 341)

In everyday discourse, then, the range of options available for incorporating another's speech into our own include many of the same devices available to the prose artist: imitation (as replication), stylization, skaz, parody, and so on. As in novelistic discourse, our "practical, everyday speech" is capable of merging with the speech of another, losing itself within the speech of another, and thereby becoming a single voice unto itself. But, as Bakhtin suggests, this fusion of voices is rather difficult to accomplish, since the introduction of "someone else's words . . . into our own speech inevitably assume[s] a new (our own) interpretation and become[s] subject to our evaluation of them; that is they become double-voiced"

(*PDP* 195). Bakhtin seems to imply that pure imitation of another's speech is possible only if the speaker is *unaware* that she is using the words of another, "forgetting whose they are" (*PDP* 195). Otherwise, a *conscious* use of someone else's speech cannot avoid the necessity of having to interpret that speech, cannot escape the exigencies of hermeneutic translation.

Further support for this view of imitation can be found in Bakhtin's theory of the utterance. If one characteristic of the utterance is its unrepeatability, then the use of someone else's words can never be a mere duplication of those words, since another's words will necessarily be recontextualized by the "host" speaker. As Bakhtin explains, "the speech of another, once enclosed in a context, is—no matter how accurately transmitted—always subject to certain semantic changes. The context embracing another's word is responsible for its dialogizing background, whose influence can be very great" (*DI* 340). The implicit suggestion here is that only sentences can be imitated, since only sentences are repeatable phenomena, a fact that results from their exclusively linguistic and, therefore, decontextualized nature. From this point of view, the history of imitation in discourse pedagogy might best be understood as the history of students imitating the sentences (not utterances) of chosen others, regardless of whether these sentences were of the spoken or written variety. Models for imitation, in this scheme of things, were never meant to be engaged, worked over, disputed, confirmed—in a word, *answered*. Rather, they were presented as reified, abstracted objects of language, whose forms were deemed worthy of replication.

However simplistic this account might be, it is important to note that Bakhtin did, in fact, address the problem of imitation in school learning, though somewhat obliquely. "When verbal disciplines are taught in school," Bakhtin observes, "two basic modes are recognized for the appropriation and transmission—simultaneously—of another's words (a text, a rule, a model): 'reciting by heart' and 'retelling in one's own words'" (*DI* 341). The first is essentially a verbatim transcription from memory and corresponds with most traditional understandings of imitation in the classroom. The second is more akin to what is usually referred to as paraphrase and is of considerable interest to Bakhtin, since it represents "on a small scale the task implicit in all prose stylistics":

> retelling a text in one's own words is to a certain extent a double-voiced narration of another's words, for indeed "one's own words" must not completely dilute the quality that makes another's words unique; a retelling in one's own words should have a mixed character, able when necessary to reproduce the style and expressions of the transmitted text. It is this second mode . . . that includes within it an entire series of forms for the appropriation while transmitting of another's words. (*DI* 341-42)

But Bakhtin does not regard these operations to be exclusively pedagogical in interest or value; rather, each strategy corresponds to separate kinds of discourse. As I noted in the last chapter, "Reciting by heart" is representative of what Bakhtin calls authoritative discourse—that is, discourse "intended to be admired, venerated, nostalgicaly invoked. It imagines itself to be eternally repeatable, and thus its authority is catechistic in nature" (*DI* 342). As I also pointed out earlier, and in contrast to authoritative discourses, "retelling in one's own words" approximates what Bakhtin calls *internally persuasive discourse,* a discourse close at hand. It is one open to appropriation by other discourses and thus one thoroughly situated *in dialogue* with those words told and retold. Internally persuasive discourse is nothing less than momentous in human development:

> Such discourse is of decisive significance in the evolution of an individual consciousness; consciousness awakens to independent ideological life precisely in a world of alien discourses surrounding it, and from which it cannot initially separate itself; the process of distinguishing between one's own and another's discourse, between one's own and another's thought, is activated rather late in development. When thought begins to work in an independent, experimenting and discriminating way, what first occurs is a separation between internally persuasive discourse and authoritarian enforced discourse, along with a rejection of those discourses that do not matter to us. (*DI* 345)

Bakhtin obviously understands the importance of a dialogic relationship with the language of the *other* to be essential to the development of individuated consciousness. Bakhtin's remarks on the nature of these relationships, moreover, suggest a resistance to those forms of imitation that exclude—or, more precisely, attempt to exclude—genuine dialogue, since such forms, by virtue of trying to fuse with another's language, exclude the possibility of relationship with that language and, hence, the full development of consciousness. This should not be understood to mean, however, that Bakhtin rejects all forms of imitation. Rather, he disparages only those that seek identity with the object of imitation, that seek a monologic unity, a merging with the language of the other. There are, of course, other kinds of imitation, many of which Bakhtin writes of approvingly.

As noted, Bakhtin is explicitly critical of those kinds of discourse that preclude dialogue, namely, authoritarian discourse, the sentence (as a purely linguistic phenomenon), and the single-voiced discourse that results from a merging of authorial and character voices. In each of these, imitation is conceived as a monologic phenomenon: it refuses the creative mingling of internally persuasive words, the answerability of utterances, the necessary distance between the languages of the stylizer and the languages stylized. Imitation, understood in its most ordinary and narrow sense, attempts to remove the voice of the other from any zone of dialogic contact, either by refusing to hear it or by becoming one with it.

But *must* imitation be a verbal strategy whose only purpose is to silence or ignore the voice of the other; must imitation, in other words, be an exclusively monologic phenomenon? The answer to this is yes, *if*—and only if—imitation is rigidly construed to be the mechanical replication (i.e., "servile copying") of another's words. As I have shown, Bakhtin has very little to say about imitation of this sort, other than to posit its existence in novelistic and everyday discourses. He is far more interested in those representations of another's language that require two or more voices, e.g., stylization, skaz, rejoinder, parody, and paraphrase. Central to my argument, of course, is the proposition that each of these may likewise be, and indeed have been, considered a *kind* of imitation; and, thus, to the extent that each is, as Bakhtin says, a form of double-voiced discourse, it is reasonable to entertain the possibility of a *dialogic imitation*. But what would be the characteristic features of such an imitation? And how might it appear in the writing classroom?

OUTLINE FOR A DIALOGIC IMITATION

In light of the discussion above, it seems possible to infer certain features of what I call here a dialogic imitation—at least enough to offer a preliminary sketch of what such an imitation might look like. Before I offer that sketch, however, I would remind that, with the possible exception of a few remarks on paraphrase, Bakhtin does not concern himself with the pedagogical implications of imitation. Though by all accounts a remarkable teacher himself, Bakhtin's scholarly interests seldom gravitated toward education and pedagogy. I also wish to point out that in calling upon Bakhtin here, my purpose in these final pages is not to propose any startling "new and improved" forms of imitation. I don't believe any such forms exist, at least none that I could hazard. But as my reconstruction of his scattered comments will show, I do believe that Bakhtin gives us some very different starting points—premises, if you like—by which to reconsider imitation.

This is a matter of some importance. As many have pointed out, there are at least two standard reasons why imitation finds little favor among compositionists. One is that imitation has been inextricably aligned with text-based rhetorics and is, therefore, bound to "product" understandings of how writing should be taught. The other is that imitation is considered unacceptable because it did not comport with expressivist, post-romantic conceptions of selfhood, with notions of the "true self" and how best to address that self in writing pedagogies.[4] Put differently, imitation in our time has been largely discredited because its premises, its starting points, have been aligned with the formalism of traditional rhetorics and because, at a crucial moment in our discipline's history, it stood in opposition to the widely endorsed expressivism of romantic and post-romantic rhetorics.

But to reject imitation according to certain assumed premises is not to reject imitation altogether. It may be that a different understanding of imitation is possible, one that derives from very different starting points, very different assumptions about knowledge, subjectivity, and language than those that authorize our current refusal to look upon imitation favorably. So then, given a specifically dialogic understanding of imitation, what are its key features?

Dialogic Imitation is Positional

Whether in novelistic or everyday discourse, when we ask of all forms of double-voicing—parody, skaz, paraphrase, hidden polemic, stylization, heteroglossia, and so on—what they have in common, the answer is that each reveals how one speaker's discourse *positions* itself toward the discourse of another, or others. In an ontological sense, for Bakhtin, the acts of positioning, orienting toward, having an attitude—these are not simple matters of choice. Even from his earliest writings, Bakhtin doubts whether it is possible to experience the world and the word in a condition of sublime neutrality. In *Toward a Philosophy of the Act,* for example, Bakhtin will repeatedly point out that words are never exclusively used to refer to the objects of the world; rather, words always express "my valuative attitude toward the object, toward what is desirable or undesirable in it" (32). Indeed, Bakhtin hints that it may be oxymoronic to talk of disinterested experience: "an object that is absolutely indifferent, totally finished," according to Bakhtin "cannot be something one actually becomes conscious of" (32).

And yet, what informs most traditional approaches to imitation is the tacit requirement that students *assume no position whatsoever* toward the modeled language, that students voice no evaluative stance toward other people's words *as words actually addressed to someone.* Rather, in a classroom of this sort, students are typically asked to imitate the "word as object" (admittedly, sublime object) or rather, the word as linguistic "matter," say, introductory participial phrases, apposition structures, figures of speech, cumulative sentences, T-unit variations, etc. For what distinguishes traditional imitation from the kind I propose here is that imitation, as it has been conventionally approached, seeks identity not difference, one voice not two, no boundaries instead of the one that allows a student to take a position toward the language of the other.

Cast in a Bakhtinian light, and as I mentioned earlier, the long history of imitation can be understood as the history of imitating sentences, not utterances. Yet if this is so, there exists no real possibility for a dialogic relationship to the language imitated. In other words, the modeled language is neither answered nor addressed, and thus any resulting imitation of that language could similarly invite no answer and address no one. The conclusion to be drawn here is that because only utterances, not sentences, seek and indeed require the voice of another, then any dialogic imitation will necessarily involve two voices. As Bakhtin says, "any truly creative voice can only be the *second* voice in a discourse" (*SG* 110), and thus dialogic imitation will ultimately require some form of double-voicing, if for no other reason than that a single voice can take no position toward itself.

Dialogic Imitation is Revisable

The process movement took as a cornerstone of its approach the notion that we cannot effectively teach writing if we attend only to the finished product, instead of to the struggles that writers experience in their working toward that finished product. Indeed, I think it safe to say our discipline was founded on the realization that there is little to teach at all if we merely evaluate written products and ignore how student writers develop and order their ideas, how they revise for their own satisfaction and for that of their audiences, how they might better proof, edit, and present their work, and so on. In more recent years, we have expanded this idea to include social and cultural processes larger than the solitary writer and her struggles, but perhaps, in some measure, determinant of each. We have also turned our attentions to the processes of texts as they make their way in a field of other texts and contexts, other writers and other readers.

In light of more recent understandings of process, then, it is not only the case that texts can be mistakenly looked upon as finished products. It is also possible to reify *attitudes toward texts*. In an odd sort of way, that is, we can make into products the very attitudes we invite our students to take toward models that we present them with. Just as product approaches to teaching composition seriously limit the likelihood of any authentic teaching at all, the same follows from any attempt to treat our students' positions toward texts as final, rigid, unchanging. Therefore, if our students have no opportunity to struggle with the language of the other, if they have no opportunity to develop new perspectives by entering into, trying on, the perspective of another, then, indeed, we have taught them little more than to be content with the immediate positions they assume, to be satisfied with their first impressions, initial reactions, and so on. It is hard to imagine this as a worthwhile pedagogical goal.

But as we have seen earlier, Bakhtin places an enormous amount of importance on the developmental value of struggle, of working through another's discourse, of "coming to terms" with the words of another, so as to assimilate those words and make them one's own. Clearly, Bakhtin understands this struggle diachronically, as a process occurring through time—in fact, one could even say through a lifetime. Yet a problem remains: How is it possible to assimilate the language or voices or perspective of another without becoming one with the other?

Again, such is possible only if we realize that developing a position toward another's words is as much a process as writing a paper in one's own words. We might be able to illuminate this point by extrapolating from Bakhtin's early work on ethics and aesthetics, where he examines the phenomenon of "live entering" and "return" and the possibility of "co-experiencing" the other from within. As always, Bakhtin is resistant to any merging of identities, to any fusion with the other. As a matter of fact, Bakhtin will claim that, despite our occasional desires for achieving such complete empathy, it is not possible to do so. "Strictly speaking," Bakhtin observes, "a pure projection of myself into the other, a move involving the loss of my own unique place outside the other is, on the whole, hardly possible; in any event, it is quite fruitless and senseless" (*AA* 26). And yet, this does not mean that there is no value whatsoever in projecting oneself into the "life-horizon" of another, the position occupied by another. How else, in fact, would understanding and empathy be possible?

In his discussion on the aesthetic relationships that obtain between authors and their "heroes," Bakhtin notes that a "first step" in aesthetic activity is one whereby an author enters into the perspective of another—a narrator, character, hero—for the purpose of understanding that other by "experiencing his life from within. . . . I must experience—come to see and know," Bakhtin says, "what *he* experiences; I must put myself in *his* place, . . . I must appropriate to myself the concrete life horizon of this human being as he experiences it himself" (*AA* 25). And yet, Bakhtin hastens to remind, this is only a first step. Whether friend or character, neighbor or narrator, we must not reside within the perspective of another. Doing so is "pathological," Bakhtin adds, unless my entering into is followed by "a *return* to my own place outside . . . for only from this place can the material derived from projecting myself into the other be rendered meaningful ethically, cognitively, or aesthetically" (*AA* 25). It is only from that place we return to, from our position outside another, that we can have any meaning for another. Or, for that matter, for ourselves.[5]

It would seem, then, that discovering one's position toward another's word is a sequenced process, a journey of repeated phases of venturing forth and return. Bakhtin's own vocabulary would suggest as much, particularly when he attempts to describe this movement in terms such as "first steps," "followed by," "actually begins," and "return." But, in fact, Bakhtin sees these two "moments" as simultaneous, insisting that they "do not follow one another chronologically," but rather are always "intimately intertwined," coupled (*AA* 27). And importantly, this simultaneity applies not merely to the other, but also to that which the other cannot be separated from, the uttered word.

> In a verbal work, every word keeps both moments in view: every word performs a twofold function insofar as it directs my projection of myself into the other as well as brings him to completion, except that one constitutive moment may prevail over the other. (*AA* 27)

Bakhtin's specific concern here is the aesthetic relationship between author and hero. But having already shown how Bakhtin rejects any absolute division between novelistic and everyday discourses, we can safely assume that Bakhtin's observations have implications beyond their more narrow formulations.

In fact, it seems to me that within our own disciplinary context, Bakhtin's ideas are echoed in the early work of Ann Berthoff, who, in calling our attention to I. A. Richards's "continuing audit of meaning," also tried to capture something of the back and forth simultaneity involved in meaning-making—or, translated to my purposes here, the process by which one assumes a position (however much it might be later revised) toward the discourse of another. David Bartholomae has also pointed to what Bakhtin is after, I think, when observing that, as our students struggle with the discourses of the university, "there are two gestures present . . . one imitative and one critical. The writer continually audits and pushes against a language that would render him 'like everyone else' and mimics the language and interpretive system of the privileged community" ("Inventing" 143). These "two gestures" are each crucial to the development of writers, each simultaneously present as writers struggle to negotiate a position within the discourses of the institution.

Thus, even though positionality is key to any understanding of a dialogic imitation, it is a positionality that is, in some sense, hard-earned, struggled for, as we appropriate and are appropriated by other people's words. In the process of this struggle, a paradox emerges: to achieve a position toward another's word, we must come to know that word, as it were, from the inside out—never completely of course, since, as Bakhtin reminds, no total merging with another's discourse is possible. But we must know the other's word enough to eventually take up a position outside and directed toward it. To know the other's word in this way, as Mary Minock suggests, may in fact be a condition for dialogue.

Dialogic Imitation is Rhetorical

Even its staunchest defenders, of course, would say that traditional imitation had very clear, rhetorical purposes—among them, to acquaint students with models of writerly excellence, to develop within students an available repertoire of styles and forms, and so on. All such purposes, however, seemed to be limited to the strictly pedagogical. But by rhetorical, I mean something more than what any given teacher might hope to accomplish by having students imitate another's models. I mean that dialogic imitation occurs within the context of some larger intention, some desire to accomplish an effect upon the world in which one's word is uttered.

Imitation, from this point of view, is hardly a passive operation, a simple parroting of someone else's words. It is, rather, something more akin to a rhetorical appropriation of another's words for one's own purposes. What, in fact, makes this appropriation rhetorical is Bakhtin's view that any speaker or writer will have purposes distinct from those to be found in the appropriated language of another speaker or writer. The rote, mechanical act of duplication for no obvious or immediate goal, the lamentable "imitation for imitation's sake" approach would find little favor with Bakhtin, since such a technique requires neither *authentic* struggle with another's language, nor demands any apparent purpose—for the student at least—beyond the fact of imitation itself. Imitation, from a Bakhtinian perspective, must have some purpose beyond itself.

And how might it be possible to illustrate the rhetorical character of a dialogic imitation? One way would be to return to that most obvious of double-voiced discourse, parody. By its very nature, parody offers a way to raise two issues of enduring concern to rhetorical instruction, namely, the importance of situational context and the significance of audience. Indeed, the writing of parody can serve as a springboard for discussions that attempt to address the problems of contexts and readers.

Of the first of these, for example, Gary Saul Morson observes that it is impossible to parody linguistic matter—say, for example, the "unit" of linguistics, the sentence. This is due to the fact that parody is always parody of an utterance, of a speech act occurring within a situational context. According to Morson, "we cannot parody words, syntax, or any other element, whether 'formal' or 'material' out of which utterances are made, but only utterances themselves, since parody cannot avoid the recontextualization of one voice by another ("Parody" 73). Parody, then, is not a comment about the linguistic features of another's word; it is a comment on the situational context in which the original voice was heard. Thus parody directs our attention away from the text "to the *occasion* (more accurately, the parodist's version of the occasion) of its *uttering*" (71). Morson explains how this is possible:

The parodist . . . aims to reveal the otherwise covert aspects of that occasion, including the unstated motives and assumptions of both the speaker and the assumed and presumably sympathetic audience. Unlike that audience, the audience of the parody is asked to consider why someone might make, and someone else entertain, the original utterance. By pointing to the unexamined presuppositions and unstated interests that conditioned the original exchange, the parodist accomplishes what Fielding calls "the discovery of affectation" . . . the divergence between professed and unacknowledged intentions—or the discovery of naiveté. (71-72)

Parody, then, is not so much linguistic play, but social commentary, an evaluation and critique of someone else's use of language in a prior situation. And as Morson also indicates, parody is thoroughly contingent on a developed sense of audience awareness.

Some of the complexities of this awareness can be apprehended through an examination of parody, because parody presumes secondary and tertiary audiences. That is, not only does the parodist address the one parodied in the parody itself, but every parody is, as Morson points out, "an interaction designed to be heard and interpreted by a third person (or second 'second' person), whose own process of active reception is anticipated and directed" (65). The parodist, to borrow Bakhtin's phrase, deploys the "word with a sidelong glance," forever conscious that his message is one addressed in at least two directions. Moreover, the parodist often invokes what is sometimes called a *conspiratorial audience,* one that is invited to something of a privileged view on a prior discourse—or even a prior audience. Indeed, in order to accomplish their intended effects, some parodies demand that the parodist's audience evaluate the audience addressed by the original.

Requiring students to write their own parodies, then, is important because, as a particularly dialogic form of imitation, it allows them the opportunity to have experience and practice in writing double-voiced discourse and, hence, an opportunity to exercise simultaneously the "two gestures" that Bartholomae refers to—one imitative, the other critical. It also (and typically) entails seeing through the eyes of another's language, and, thus, requires the kind of continual shifting in perspective that Bakhtin might applaud. But finally, as I have tried to show here, parody is useful because it offers an excellent way to broach some of the complexities of three enduring staples of rhetorical education: context, audience, and purpose.

IMITATION, IMAGINATION, AND DIALOGUE

While I have taken some pains to show how Bakhtin might ask us to rethink imitation, and while I have tried to enunciate some general features of what such an imitation would consist of, I have avoided offering classroom activities and exercises, assignments, guidelines, pointers, etc. In one sense, I doubt whether it is necessary to do so. Having co-authored an extensive review of the literature on imitation, I can attest to no shortage of imaginative approaches to imitative pedagogies. The only shortage I can discern is that few scholars in rhetoric and composition have seriously attempted to develop classroom pedagogies that understand imitation dialogically.[6]

This is unfortunate in my view. Bakhtin's theories of dialogue, I think, have the potential to free us of our conventional ideas about imitation—and conventional ideas about why it ought to be rejected. Bakhtin would remind us that our present certainties, even those regarding imitation, are likely to become canonized, routinized, and that we therefore might be wise to eschew any and all last word pronouncements about anything. "Nothing is absolutely dead," Bakhtin tells us, "every meaning will have its homecoming festival" (SG 170). Could this be true, even of imitation?

I do not know the answer to that question. Perhaps, despite the judgments of Corbett and Connors, imitation will someday make a comeback. Whether or not this comes to pass, I happen to believe that Bakhtin's ideas may already help us understand why imitation was a centerpiece of language instruction through centuries past. I also happen to believe that Bakhin's ideas could possibly challenge us to develop pedagogies that find a place for imitation in the future, but only an imitation understood dialogically. I have tried to offer a few signposts along this pathway.

5 PICTURES AT AN EXHIBITION
Bakhtin, Composition, and the Problem of the Outside

> Public speech is a performance in time, located at specific historical junctures, temporary and unstable, even though it is imagined as a location in space, always available, with secure and discernable borders.
>
> *Susan Wells*

> For us, the social force of time is not a source of hope but a specter promising the degeneration of all that we can still value. The challenge then is to show why we need a temporal dimension to our interpretive thinking.
>
> *Charles Altieri*

Of the many Bakhtinian ideas that have found currency among scholars and teachers in composition—voice, heteroglossia, carnival, dialogue, to name the most obvious—one idea that has not commanded much attention is Bakhtin's notion of "outsidedness." This is a bit surprising, since Bakhtin alludes to it in many of his major works, from his very early fragment, *Toward a Philosophy of the Act*, to his very late essay, "Response to a Question from *Novy Mir*." Bakhtin continually emphasizes the importance of having, maintaining, and exercising an outside perspective—whether that perspective occurs in relationships between self and other, author and character, or culture and culture.

Of these, in fact, the relationship that perhaps best illuminates outsidedness is the one that occurs between self and other. For a thinker who understood selfhood largely as a gift bestowed from the other, we can easily glimpse why Bakhtin places so much importance on outsidedness. In his own terms, an outside perspective provides one with an "excess of seeing" or "surplus of vision" that the other cannot provide for herself. My vision of the other, in a sense, completes the other—or at least attempts to—because I can see what he or she cannot. Elaborating on this point, Bakhtin says,

> I shall always see and know something that he, from his place outside and over against me, cannot see himself: parts of his body that are inaccessible to his own gaze (his head, his face and its expression), the world behind his back, and a whole series of objects and relations which in any of our mutual relations are accessible to me but not to him. As we gaze at each other, two different worlds are reflected in the pupils of our eyes. (AA 23)

Bakhtin chooses a visual metaphor here to suggest the crucial importance of the other to the self I understand myself to be. Indeed, Bakhtin will say it is because of the other's "seeing, remembering, gathering, and unifying self-activity" that I am able to construct an identity at all. Or, as Bakhtin puts it, an "outward personality could not exist, if the other did not create it" (AA 36).

Given the rather profound responsibilities, then, that the self has toward the other, the self must resist any temptation to merge, to become one, to completely empathize with the other. In a famous passage that speaks to this particular feature of outsidedness, Bakhtin asks,

> In what way would it enrich the event if I merged with the other. . . . And what would I myself gain by the other's merging with me? . . . Let him rather remain outside of me, for in that position he can see and know what I myself do not see and do not know from my own place, and he can essentially enrich the event of my own life. (AA 88)

Therefore, we should not seek identity with the other, for to achieve such a condition would be to negate the possibility of a *relationship* with the other. Take away our mutual outsidedness, and we will not mean anything to each other at all.

Now, I would like to register two criticisms of Bakhtin's outsidedness, the first of which I am merely reiterating because it is so commonly heard. Bakhtin seems to imagine the outsider's perspective as always kindly, benevolent, affirming, generous, and gift-bestowing. He seems, in other words, not to acknowledge the outsider's gaze as potentially hostile or threatening, the outsider's gaze as something perceived to be less than providential. My second criticism, one that I will return to in my closing, has to do with the implications of thinking about outsidedness in exclusively spatial terms. Certainly, the term itself suggests that we must do so. But it seems to me that without a temporal dimension to the notion of outsidedness, we would have no way of disputing whatever outside perspective we encounter. Or, to put the same point in Bakhtin's more familiar dialogic terms, without time we would have no way of *answering* what others see. Thus, the notion of pure outsidedness could imply an autonomy of perspective, sufficient beyond any need for dialogic response. Yet such a conclusion would gainsay nearly everything Bakhtin wrote about the utterance in particular and dialogue in general.

THREE REPRESENTATIONS, THREE RESPONSES

As mentioned, I'll return to this latter point toward the end of this chapter, but for now, I would like to attempt to "answer" three highly unflattering outside perspectives on composition. As with many such representations of contemporary writing instruction, the ones I will discuss here are unabashedly hostile to what we do. In that sense, they not only offer representations of composition, but, taken together, they themselves represent widespread attitudes among the public at large about how writing is taught and who teaches it—attitudes that are overwhelmingly negative.

In order, then, I will first examine a snippet that appeared in *Harper's Magazine* in 1994 entitled "Reading, Writing, Rambling On," an excerpt from an interview with Victor Vitanza that originally appeared in *Composition Studies*. I will follow Vitanza's excerpt with an article by the former chair of a high school English department, written for and published in the *San Francisco Chronicle*. I will conclude with what is by far the most elaborate—and scathing—indictment of all, a chapter entitled "Croaking about Comp" from Terry Caesar's *Conspiring with Forms: Life in Academic Texts*. First, then, the Vitanza excerpt.

What strikes one most upon reading this excerpt is how thoroughly in keeping it is with the tenor established by the now-famous *Harper's Index,* which opens every issue. There, as many know, the reader is presented with a list of seemingly random facts, statistics, items, all of which are meant not merely to provide information but also to inspire a laugh, a moment of amazement or wonder, perhaps even a fleeting instant of outrage. Typically, the intended effect is elicited by juxtaposing one item with a (loosely) related other item, thereby inviting the reader to make a comparison and eventual conclusion. For this to work, the reader must "fill in the blanks," so to speak, by tacitly agreeing to the assumptions of those who compile the list, a requirement that makes the whole process of reading the *Index* a highly enthymematic one.

The same is true of the Vitanza snippet. As with the *Index,* no comment is deemed necessary or, for that matter, desirable. What *Harper's* attempts to do is simply offer a brief, verbatim excerpt from an interview with Vitanza that intends (I would assume) to characterize him as incoherent, pretentious, and something of a bore. To illustrate what I mean, I quote here a portion of the excerpt that appeared in *Harper's*:

> *Cynthia Haynes-Burton:* Who do you think your audience is?
> *Victor Vitanza:* My attitudes are that I am very much a "comp teacher," that I am a writing instructor, and that I am contemplative about what I do. I always am giving writing lessons. I don't know, however, if I am Levi-Strauss or if I am that South American Indian chief in *Tristes Tropiques* that Levi-Strauss indirectly gives writing lessons to. Perhaps I am both. Which can be confusing. . . . One of the fundamental questions that I am ever-reflexively confronted with is that I do not know who I am for this profession. . . .
> *Cynthia Haynes-Burton:* Please start over.
> *Victor Vitanza:* Okay, so what I have said so far: I very consciously do not follow the field's research protocols. And yet, of course, I do; most other times, I do not. And yet again! Do you feel the vertigo of this? (Haynes-Burton 51)

Now, to have to explain the Vitanza excerpt is like having to explain the punch line to a joke—once you've reached that point, real laughter becomes, well, nearly impossible. But, then, the question remains: what exactly is it that *Harper's* needs its readers to think in order for us to enjoy this excerpt in the way intended? In trying to answer that question, I've developed a list of assumptions that, I believe, *Harper's* would like its readers to endorse:

- That Victor Vitanza is the representative *par excellence* of all scholars who work in the field of composition studies and, quite probably, the entire contemporary Academy;

- That, yes, the contemporary Academy is going to hell in a handbasket, Vitanza being a prime example of its imminent decline;

- That more evidence of this decline can be inferred from the fact that an entire specialty devoted to freshman composition exists at all and that Vitanza is one of its luminaries;

- That, because of his obvious, insistent, seemingly nonsensical ramblings, Vitanza ought not to be teaching anyone how to write;

- That logic, clarity, coherence, in contrast to Vitanza's ramblings, are the hallmarks of good writing; these are the *Ur* values of the written word and therefore ought never to be compromised;

- That publishing a 250-word excerpt from a 17-page interview in no way compromises the logic, clarity, and coherence of the original author's discourse;

- That there can be no alternative to understanding what language does except through these values.

Regardless of how each of us might position our own work in relation to Vitanza's, few of us would abide the view that the presentation of his scholarship is either (1) all that representative of the scholarly approaches of his colleagues or (2) utterly devoid of sense (though, to be sure, Vitanza will press us to question our ordinary ideas of what is sensical). If we wanted to determine for ourselves whether or not *Harper's* gave a fair picture of Vitanza in this interview, most of us would probably read the original interview in *Composition Studies*—admittedly a task somewhat easier for us than for the general reader of *Harper's*.

And yet, what we would find upon reading the interview in *Composition Studies*, however, is a full frontal attack on the discursive values that *Harper's* holds dear. Among other things, Vitanza launches into a critique of Enlightenment *logos,* sensing that within our irrational faith in the superrational, there lurks a menacing foundationalism that is implicitly associated with imperialist and colonialist impulses. Arguments that proceed on Enlightenment logos, that is, arguments that embrace facile notions of logic, clarity, and coherence, are, in Vitanza's view of things, dangerous, heavy-handed, and enormously self-deluding. As he himself points out in the interview, "people who speak or write in impeccably clear language are the greatest of liars, whether they know it or not" (57). Vitanza mocks those delusions.

Along the way, he also mocks the genre of the interview. He does so (1) by beginning the interview with a question that *he* puts to the interviewer; (2) by dodging nearly all subsequent questions put to him; (3) by calling into question the very act of questioning: and (4) by including in his answers that distinctive manner of stylistic irreverence that we have come to expect of Vitanza: abundant word play, intentional misspellings, typographic heresies, unconventional hyphenations—all of which, taken together, spoof the commonly accepted idea that published interviews are (or in any way could be) faithful transcriptions of what someone else said. In short, but in practically all respects, Vitanza parodies the very criteria by which *Harper's* wants us to judge him—logic, clarity, and coherence. But how could the usual reader of *Harper's* possibly know this?

In an E-mail to Robert Connors (and later distributed to subscribers of the H-Net History of Rhetoric discussion group), Vitanza gives his own response to the *Harper's* excerpt, a remarkably non-defensive rejoinder to, as he puts it, being "enframed." He notes that "what the interview is all about [is] how Victor . . . avoids questions and yet responds to them," a reflexivity that would no doubt escape readers who knew nothing of Vitanza, his work, or the interview from which the excerpt was taken. He also recognizes a certain anxiety that could likely be felt in the profession, an anxiety that might be paraphrased thus: "Oh, my God, what will people think of the rest of us . . . in rhetoric and composition . . . if they think we are like V? No wonder why Dick and Jane can't write no mo!" Vitanza sympathizes with colleagues who might feel this way, but since he, too, is against (that is, both contrary to and alongside of) mainline colleagues in composition, he cannot worry too much about how readers of *Harper's* choose to see him or the field. In light of these remarks, it seems reasonable to conclude that *Harper's* is far more threatened and defensive about what Vitanza represents to *Harper's* than what *Harper's* represents to Vitanza.

But what about the rest of us—those "mainline colleagues" of Vitanza's whose everyday practices are not likely to command the attention of *Harper's*, whose stated words may not be provocative enough for mass scrutiny and thus mass ridicule. We, too, are subject to public criticism, though such criticism is usually directed toward us as a group (the collective of "English teachers") and not as individuals. A recent example of this particular brand of criticism can be found in David Ruenzel's, "The Write Way to Success: 'Feel Good' Writing Deprives Students of Needed Skills." Ruenzel's opinion piece appeared in the *San Francisco Chronicle*.

Ruenzel begins by recounting the story of a time when he chaired a high school English department and was summoned by his principal for a conference. During their talk, the principal told Ruenzel that he needed to give more attention to how students might achieve a sense of "emotional commitment" to their writing, a needed sense of "ownership." The principal suggested that Ruenzel's "insistence that they develop a thesis and use proper English made them feel that their work no longer 'belonged to them.'" Ruenzel's essay is a response to what he regards as the process orthodoxies embraced by his principal and demanded by the profession at large.

Identifying "ownership" as "a central tenet" of the process movement, Ruenzel proceeds to link an array of other—in his opinion, misguided—practices to process orthodoxy: the "quasi-therapeutic" aims of exploratory discourse, naturalistic learning models, collaboration, student-centered pedagogies, and the widespread acceptance of "feel-good" writing instruction. In their place, Ruenzel advocates a return to "rigorous academic standards in the language arts." Ruenzel even hints that students know—and resent—how precious little is being demanded of them. According to Ruenzel, students whom he once taught at a local commuter college implored him not "to put us in any more writing groups. Teach us to write a thesis statement."

Now it must be asked, what does such a request tell us about those students' previous experience with formal writing pedagogy? To request instruction on how to write a thesis statement, after all, assumes that the person making such a request already knows *something* about what a thesis statement is or what it's supposed to do. Such a request implies, moreover, that the person asking must have some notion, however vague, that the ability to write a thesis statement has something to do with the ability to write well. Yet, how or where could such views be acquired, if not through prior writing instruction?

It is possible, I suppose, to imagine a parent or other close family member advising a younger relative to demand to be taught how to write a thesis statement. It is even possible to imagine some process-oriented teacher extolling the virtues of thesis statements but refusing to teach them, thereby leaving his or her students feeling cheated, bereft of valuable knowledge that would help them to improve their writing. The latter seems quite a stretch, though, unless we want to suggest that some process teachers are not only misinformed but intentionally cruel. No, what's most likely, I think, is that Ruenzel's students have already had instruction in writing thesis statements and have decided, for whatever reasons, that they need more. But since Ruenzel finds it remarkably easy to blame process methods for the sorry state of writing that he routinely encounters, then, by his own logic, traditional instruction in skills must be, in some measure, implicated in this failure as well. Otherwise, why didn't those students—the ones who almost certainly received *some* instruction in writing thesis statements—turn out to be the kind of students Ruenzel claims they would? And why, then, wouldn't Ruenzel see fit to assign some degree of blame to traditional pedagogies for their apparent failure?

The answer, it seems to me, is that Ruenzel has too much invested in the either-or logic of his position. In order to make this kind of argument, Ruenzel has to consolidate all extant teaching practices into two opposing camps—process and traditional—conveniently ignoring the profound differences of opinion that exist *within* those separate camps, the commonalities they might share with each other, and, for that matter, any alternate explanations for what Ruenzel sees as the dire state of current writing instruction.

Thus, to offer an obvious example, Ruenzel makes no mention of the rather fierce disagreements that emerged among process advocates during the 1980s and well into the 1990s. Nor does he mention that the process movement, from its inception, had its critics and detractors from within the ranks of English teachers. Nor does he mention the eloquent and forceful critiques of process theory offered by, among others, Lisa Delpit—to wit, that process approaches reflect white, middle-class assumptions about learning and language. Nor does he acknowledge that at the time his piece appeared, a good deal of discussion centered upon whether or not composition studies had moved into what Thomas Kent and Sidney Dobrin call a *post*-process era. Of course, within the profession, there is indeed wide agreement that process approaches marked a significant advance over the current-traditional approaches that they sought to replace. But to represent the "process" movement as a seamless whole, dogmatically imposed or endorsed, is a gross simplification.

Perhaps an even greater simplification is Ruenzel's assumption that a facile, unmediated, simple cause and effect relationship exists between writing pedagogy and writing ability. Scholars as diverse as Mina Shaughnessey, Patricia Bizzell, James Berlin, Mike Rose, and Walter Ong have all, in often very different ways, relieved us of this notion by showing how teaching practices always occur within larger historical and cultural contexts. Whether mapping the characteristics of secondary orality; or noting the enormous changes resulting from open admissions in colleges and universities; or exposing the varied interests served by recurrent literacy crises, or chronicling the shifting demographics of the American populace and the increased linguistic diversity that such shifts entailed— regardless, some of the best work to emerge out of the process movement was conducted by scholars who (somewhat ironically in my view) undermined the naive belief that "teaching process" could wholly determine, or otherwise account for, writing ability. Ruenzel's wish to blame process teaching for the utter demise of written literacy is a wish that simply cannot afford to acknowledge the complexities brought to light by the kinds of scholarly inquiries mentioned here. For Ruenzel to recognize these complexities would be to evaluate the process movement more judiciously, to see it as something other than a pedagogical scapegoat.

Finally, I would like to mention an essay by Terry Caesar entitled "Croaking about Comp." Caesar is an English professor at Clarion College in Pennsylvania who has written extensively on professional concerns and issues. His essay appears as a chapter in his collection, *Conspiring with Forms.*

Now, it would hardly be an overstatement to observe that Caesar loathes composition, not to mention the freshmen who are required to take it. On the opening page of his chapter, he tells us that he's taught two sections of comp for nearly twenty years and that only recently—the last year, in fact—has he gotten a reprieve from the stultifying drudgery that composition is. He tells us that he hopes never to have to teach comp again, for, quite candidly, he "hate[s] comp" and wonders "why the sheer detestation for teaching this subject on the freshman level never gets expressed at all" (69). Doesn't anyone else hate comp too, we can almost hear him plead, incredulous that the seeming answer to this question must be no, since no one appears to be very forthcoming. He suspects, of course, widespread dishonesty about that apparent "no."

To provide just a taste of Caesar's revulsion toward composition, I offer this sampler of random comments from his essay:

> Composition themes comprise the most massively *mindless* writing I've ever read—and read, and read. (70)

> Can it actually be true that no one who teaches comp tries to write about how empty it is as a subject or even how it gets more theoretically empowered as it gets more empty? My supposition is that no one can revile comp without immediately being accused of reviling students, who are in turn, a "god term" so professionally ceremonialized that they can only be comprehended from within the temple; furthermore anyone who doesn't approach in the right spirit must be sent packing as a person who didn't belong anyway and never believed. Comp teachers include some of the most pious, not to say evangelistic, people I've ever met. (72)

> I hate comp because at the center of teaching it there is always a moment when I don't want to be benevolent, and I hate the pretense that I have to

try to be. Sometimes this moment suggests to me that the whole enterprise is all pretense—professionalized patience, insincere concern, bored
judgment, and sheer disgust. (76)

Nearly twenty years, and I still don't know how anyone can learn anything
teaching comp, except more ways to teach comp. (81)

What can be said in response to these words? Well, to be fair,
Caesar is not altogether unfamiliar with the literature of composition
studies. He cites, among other sources, Donald Murray, Howard
Tinberg, Dana Heller, Michael Carter, and *Rhetoric Review's* "Burkean
Parlor" and refers to these sources often approvingly. He seems to
embrace a "two realms" conception of composition's professional
geography—one, the proletariat, the great wash of instructors beaten
down, hopelessly despairing, lost in reams of insipid freshman prose,
and, two, a much smaller group of instructors invigorated by the
opportunity to theorize that same prose and intrigued by how it
might be theorized even more completely. In fact, Caesar hints that
the latter group might provide the only true motivation for teaching
comp at all. As he says, "I'm now more certain than I've ever been that
all of its [composition's] many, mundane occasions can be of
immense theoretical provocation, and this can provide enough motivation—it can even provide a career—to enable just about anyone to
plow through another week's set of themes" (81).

Perhaps we ought not to react too hastily to the Great Divide that
Caesar perceives, though we may want to avoid his more extreme char-
acterizations. After all, some in our field—Sharon Crowley and David
Jolliffe come to mind—have actively promoted the abolishment of the
first-year requirement altogether. Their reasons are far different from
the ones we assume Caesar might offer, but I think he would suspect
that the motivations of the "new abolitionists" camouflage a certain
wish to be rid of comp entirely in order to better pursue what he refers
to as comp's "escape into theory," a situation where *all* may participate
in rarefied, intellectual pursuits *about* composition and no one has to
tend the fields, so to speak—no one has to *teach* composition.
Certainly, this trend has been commented upon recently by David
Bartholomae and others, who warn of the disastrous consequences of a

two realms or "two nations" model for composition ("Composition").
But whereas Caesar might find this state of affairs, by his own logic,
inevitable, Bartholomae does not.

While we might applaud Caesar for perceiving a trend that those
"inside" composition perceive as well, we also need to recall that
Caesar suspects a hefty measure of dishonesty among compositionists who never have a bad, disparaging, unhappy, or just plain tired
word to say about teaching comp. But even allowing for the calcu-
lated reticence that Caesar ascribes to us, do we—those of us trained
in teaching composition—have an exclusive purchase on disingenu-
ous silence? Caesar, for example, would have readers believe that his
views about composition originate solely from his experience of
teaching composition. This strikes me as surprising, to say the least.
Caesar, after all, is quite insightful when exploring the determining
forces at play in the institutional, theoretical, and professional questions that he addresses throughout the remainder of this collection
and in subsequent works. Yet, he wants the reader to believe that his
own attitudes toward composition have nothing to do with his graduate training, have nothing to do with his twenty or so years of professional experience in an English department, have nothing to do
with public opinions about writing instruction, and so on. He wants
us to believe, in other words, that his attitudes are immune to the very
forces—especially those forces underwritten by institutional and professional hierarchies—that have a determining effect on the rest of us,
that give rise to, among other things, the somewhat defensive zealotry
among compositionists that he cannot understand. He wants us to
believe, moreover, that in certain institutional contexts, "croaking
about comp" isn't without its rewards—isn't, in fact, a happily
indulged pastime, as it sometimes is in many departments.

These same essentializing moves are manifest in his attitudes
toward the hapless freshman writer. Since he makes no mention of
insipid prose among students taking advanced composition or
upper-division literature classes, we are left to conclude that, well,
somehow freshmen must get better—better at learning, better at
thinking, better at writing. If that's the case, then Caesar has thank-
fully avoided the temptation to indulge yet another tiresome

condemnation of an entire generation. But if freshmen improve, if their writing gets better, might their comp courses have something to do with that improvement? And if freshmen improve, ought not we conclude that blaming them for their wretched prose is tantamount to blaming them for being young, inexperienced—for being, in a word, freshmen?

In a telling passage, and one relevant to my larger purposes here, Caesar quotes a representation of the composition classroom that appeared in a recent novel. As might be expected, the novel provides yet another damning portrayal of the freshman student. But in an odd self-contradiction, Caesar comments that such portrayals "would only appear in a work of fiction because writers are outsiders to teaching. They utter the truth of outsiders—that which should not be uttered—and they utter it shamelessly" (73).

Here we have reached the opposite point on our compass. Where Bakhtin, perhaps naively, sees the outsider as one who showers beneficent gifts upon others, completing what they cannot not see of themselves, Caesar sees the outsider as one whose truths are so severe as to render those truths unspeakable, or if spoken, not without some requisite shame from the speaker, except perhaps those speakers who are writers of fiction. In any event, Caesar's notion of outsidedness is seemingly just as limited as Bakhtin's when we attempt to think of the outside dialogically, that is, when we think of how we may answer what others see of us.

PROBLEMS OF DIALOGIC OUTSIDEDNESS

At the outset, I mentioned two apparent weaknesses with Bakhtin's concept of "outsidedness." The first, a commonly heard criticism, is that Bakhtin seems to posit the outsider's gaze as one that is always benevolent, forever insightful, edifying, and redemptive. In light of the outside perspectives I discuss here, such would seem to be a hard case to make. Each of the views above is very critical of composition studies and, in the case of Caesar, enthusiastically hostile. How then may we say that composition benefits from, or is otherwise illuminated by, what any of these three perspectives offer? What gifts do the perspectives outlined here bestow?

Perhaps the only way to imagine how the outside perspectives elaborated above could benefit composition is to regard each perspective as the occasion for self-scrutiny, as prompts for questions we might not otherwise put to ourselves. In fact, there is evidence in his late writings that Bakhtin did, indeed, try to think of outsidedness this way. In a passage that tries to outline the meeting of distinct cultures, for example, Bakhtin writes:

> It is only in the eyes of *another* culture that foreign culture reveals itself fully and profoundly. . . . A meaning only reveals its depth once it has encountered and come into contact with another, foreign meaning: they engage in a kind of a dialogue . . . which surmounts the closedness and one-sidedness of these particular meanings, these cultures. We raise new questions for a foreign culture, ones that it did not raise itself; we seek answers to our own questions in it; and the foreign culture responds to us by revealing to us its new aspects and new semantic depths. (*SG* 7)

Again, we notice Bakhtin's guiding assumption, namely, that encounters with outside perspectives are always neighborly, urging us to question ourselves in ways that will eventually prove mutually illuminating. And yet, none of the critics I discuss here seem especially interested in putting questions *to* composition, though each seems very concerned with shaping views *about* composition. In fact, if any questions arise at all, they will be questions that we put to ourselves based on how we choose to interpret what our critics say. Thus, to achieve Bakhtin's version of benign outsidedness, we must translate some rather blistering portrayals of who we are and what we do into the occasion for serious, disciplinary self-examination. That can be done, of course, and there is no doubt considerable value in this very sort of self-questioning, even when prompted by less than friendly others. But the responses we develop to our own questions—are they truly answers *for us?* Or are they meant for our outside auditors, who, it must be remembered, never asked these questions of us to begin with? Bakhtin seems to suggest that in answering such questions, we can reveal "new aspects and new semantic depths" to our outsiders. But if our outsiders did not address these questions to us in the first place, and if the gaze of our outsiders is an unrelievedly critical one, might not those "new aspects and new semantic depths" risk becoming little more than apologies on our part, mere justifications for why we do what we do?

I raise these problems to emphasize the second weakness of Bakhtin's idea of outsidedness, namely, the extent to which it is, or can be, regarded as a truly dialogic concept. Even Bakhtin seems to have some reservations on this point, describing the encounter between two cultures above as *"a kind of* dialogue" (my emphasis). Bakhtin holds something back here, I think, not simply because of the formidable difficulties involved in imagining the meeting between two cultures as analogous to the meeting between two interlocutors. He holds back also because he realizes that the twin foundations of his theory of the utterance—addressivity and answerability—are both potentially compromised when regarded in light of his theory of outsidedness. As noted above, for example, an outside perspective need not be addressed to insiders at all—and indeed often is not. Yet even when not addressed to us, Bakhtin suggests that an outside perspective is capable of revealing a culture to itself through the process of internalization whereby an outside perspective becomes the motive for disciplinary self-scrutiny—that is, for questions we're more likely to address to ourselves than to our outsiders. As before, it must be asked whether any utterance (remark, question, comment, criticism) not addressed to us and answers not sought from us amount to anything even faintly resembling a dialogic exchange.

Yes, there is enormous value in self-examination—the kind of questioning, that is, that occurs *within* individuals, communities, and cultures. And surely interior dialogue is crucial to a full understanding of Bakhtinian dialogics. But it must be recalled that for Bakhtin (as for Vygotsky) interior dialogue *follows from* social dialogue; it is a product of the dialogues we *first* conduct with our others. And yet, where no authentic social dialogue is manifest—where no questions are addressed to us and no answers are sought from us—would we not be wise to consider what manner of interior dialogue could possibly derive from the sorts of outside perspectives that composition studies routinely encounters from its critics? How, then, can it be that Bakhtin's implied mutuality of perspectives is necessarily dialogic? True, in strictly dyadic terms, you are my outsider as much as I am yours. Yet, beyond the brute fact of our respective positions, there seems to be no way to explain how we might engage in dialogue with one another. In other words, and as things stand conceptually, there seems to be no particular requirement that one outside perspective need *address* another and no provision for the likelihood that one outside perspective might wish to *answer*, or be answered by, another.

When addressivity and answerability are depleted in this way, so too are the conditions for genuine dialogue. What's missing in Bakhtin's formulation of the outside—what makes outsidedness such a hard concept to square with dialogue—is precisely that certain kind of mutuality that allows for address and response, the kind of mutuality that requires *time*. Bakhtin is obviously aware that those to whom an outside perspective is directed simultaneously provide an outside perspective for those who look upon them. And he also acknowledges the mutual benefits that should result from the mere fact of our relational positioning to one another.

But then, what? What are the possibilities for dialogue once an outside perspective is announced or otherwise made known? Doesn't the very concept of outsidedness imply that an outside view need merely remain fixed in place to be legitimate, sufficient for no other reason than the fact that it exists somewhere on the outside? And, if exempt from any and all temporal considerations, how can an outside perspective ever change—or, speaking more pragmatically, how could we effect a change in how outsiders view us?

As I mentioned in my opening, we need to think about outsidedness not merely in spatial terms, but in temporal ones as well—or more precisely, in the conjunction of both terms together. Another way to put this is that we need to consider outsidedness *chronotopically*, Bakhtin's term for the unity of space and time. Without the inclusion of some temporal dimension to Bakhtin's concept of outsidedness, it will seemingly remain one of the least dialogic in his entire corpus, if for no other reason than this: strictly spatial thinking cannot account for a dialogic understanding of meaning.

TOWARD A PRAGMATIC UNDERSTANDING OF OUTSIDEDNESS

At what distance does one qualify as having an outside perspective? Are all outside perspectives equidistant from the insiders they comment upon? If not, how do those variations in distance bear upon what they see? If one outside position is exchanged for another, how does this substitution alter or determine what is seen? Moreover, what is the process by which such exchanges might occur? To put the same question a bit differently, what is the process by which an outsider might be encouraged to adopt a new perspective? Or, even more dramatically perhaps, how is it that outsiders might become insiders, or vice versa?

Because questions such as these presuppose movement and change, they seem to require a dialogic understanding of positionality Bakhtin does not provide. To answer such questions, as well as to address the problems of dialogue I have raised above, Bakhtin's outsidedness must be extended in ways that restore the temporal to the spatial, a yoking that dialogue requires. Otherwise, it must be shown that positionality—or to be more exact, *interpretive positionality*—is in fact already in time, is in fact already dialogic, and cannot escape being so. I believe that the latter is true and that the dialogic nature of Bakhtin's outsidedness can be revealed through an application of C. S. Peirce's triadic theory of meaning.

At the outset, though, it must be admitted that a fully elaborated version of Peirce's theory would not be possible here. Most of Peirce's concepts fit, or attempt to fit, within a complex system of ideas that is nothing short of daunting in its range. Peirce will variously address problems of logic and mathematics, semiotics and pragmatism, science and phenomenology, metaphysics and God—and will do so with an eye cast toward the systematic, philosophical connections that may obtain among such global areas of inquiry. Moreover, Peirce, like Bakhtin, frequently tends to revise earlier formulations of certain ideas, sometimes introducing such revisions in contexts where they might not be expected. For these reasons, I will try to limit my discussion to how a certain understanding of his triadic theory of meaning might help illuminate the problem I have set forth above.[1]

The basis of Peirce's theory is that all meaning is representation in signs and that all signs are composed of three essential terms: first, a *representamen,* or what is typically meant by "sign" in its most ordinary usage, a word, gesture, symbol, etc., that stands for, or otherwise points to, something else; second, an *object,* a term roughly equivalent to "referent," or that which is stood for or pointed to; and most importantly, Peirce's third term, an *interpretant,* or mediating idea, a constituent term of any sign and a term without which no meaning relationship is possible between representamen and its object. Peirce observes that "a *Sign,* or *Representamen,* is a First which stands in such a genuine triadic relationship to a Second, called its *Object,* as to be capable of determining a Third, called its *Interpretant,* to assume the same triadic relation to its Object in which it stands itself to the same Object" (*Collected* 2:274).

Now, it is tempting to regard the interpretant as a person, as someone who endows the otherwise meaningless relationship between representamen and object with significance. But this is not exactly what Peirce means. It would be more accurate to say that the interpretant is that idea evoked in the mind of another by which the other may similarly represent the original object. Whether or not, or how faithfully, the other chooses to outwardly represent the same object is rather beside the point. What matters is that he or she must first be able to *re*-represent the same object, in like manner, as a precondition for an appropriate response to the original sign. In Peirce's theory of meaning, this assumes that "an appropriate response," however defined by circumstances, is itself "always already" interpretive, is itself triadic in nature. As Peirce puts it, any sign "creates in the mind of [some] person an equivalent sign, or perhaps a more developed sign. That sign which it creates I call the *interpretant* of the first sign" (*Collected* 2:228). In other words, that which interprets a sign must be a sign itself.

Again, notice that while Peirce is reluctant to equate the interpretant with a person, he is far from implying that "signs interpret one another without involving persons at all" (Mounce 25). Though it will seem otherwise at times, Peirce is not offering us a theory of disembodied meaning.[2] To say, along with Peirce, that signs cannot mean apart from their relations with other signs is not to say that persons are inessential to a triadic theory of meaning. This point is best explained by W. B. Gallie in his elaboration of Peirce's definition:

> (i) A sign stands for (ii) an object by (iii) stimulating some organism or person to (iv) some appropriate response which is (v) itself capable of signifying the object of the original sign. (120)

Peirce simply dispenses with steps (iii) and (iv) because he considers both already to be implied by his more abbreviated definition.

What, then, are the broader implications of Peirce's definition, especially as those implications might relate to dialogue? First, since every sign depends upon another sign for its interpretation, it follows that there can be no first sign, just as for Bakhtin, there can be no first word. Likewise, it also follows that we never originate meaning with our utterances. Yes, obviously we extend, revise, answer, interpret, and often act upon meanings communicated to us, but, for Peirce, we would not be able to do so unless we were, in some way, already *in* meaning. Having established that "we have no power of thinking without signs" (*Collected* 5:265), Peirce will make this point in a striking analogy: "Just as we say that a body is in motion, and not that motion is in a body we ought to say that we are in thought, and not that thoughts are in us" (*Collected* 5:289n). Bakhtin, of course, would say much the same about dialogue.

A second implication of Peirce's semiotics is that every sign characteristically possesses the quality of *addressivity*. For Peirce, a sign "addresses somebody"—a not especially surprising fact given the requirement that one sign needs another for its interpretation (*Collected* 2:228). Indeed, it is through Peirce—and his insistence that speech always entails the *re*-representation of a prior sign—that we come to see the relationship between the word and the sign. Though neither Peirce nor Bakhtin develop this concept at length, it is apparent that addressivity is a feature of Peirce's triadic theory of meaning, as it is for Bakhtin's theory of the utterance. When, for example, Peirce (presaging George Herbert Mead) claims that thought is internal dialogue, he is thereby (and simultaneously) making the claim that "a person is not absolutely an individual," since internal dialogue requires a plurality of selves:

His thoughts are what he is "saying to himself," that is, saying to that other self that is just coming into life in the flow of time. When one reasons, it is that critical self that one is trying to persuade; and all thought whatsoever is a sign, and is mostly of the nature of language. The second thing to remember is that the man's circle of society (however widely or narrowly this phrase may be understood), is a sort of loosely compacted person, in some respects of higher rank than the person of an individual organism. (*Collected* 5:421)

Here, Peirce offers a sort of surprising inversion that illustrates his preference for continuities over polarities. That is, what we conventionally think of as uniform and singular—namely, interior experience—turns out instead to be a locus of pluralities, while what we typically regard as diverse or plural—namely, outward, social experience—may, at least for purposes of addressed thought, be regarded as singular, that is, as "a loosely compacted person."

Thought, then, as internal dialogue, is addressed to "that other" self, that emerging "critical" self one is trying to persuade. Elsewhere, Peirce will say that a "good introspector" must admit "that his deliberations took a dialogic form, the arguer of any moment appealing to the reasonableness of the *ego* of the succeeding moment for his critical assent" (*Essential* 402). And since Peirce regards it as obvious that "conversation is composed of signs," we are left to conclude that thought, whether conceived as internal or external dialogue, is thus always addressed to the mind of a "somebody," to another interpreter (*Essential* 402). Even in those seeming cases where "a sign has no interpreter," where no addressed interpreter is apparently present, "its interpretant is a 'would-be,' i.e., is what it *would* determine in the interpreter if there were one" (*Essential* 409).

This mention of a subjunctive conditional, of a posited "would-be" leads us to the third and most compelling reason why dialogue is implied by a Peircean semiotics. In brief, Peirce's conditional illustrates an important way in which his theory of meaning relates to his more encompassing theory of pragmatism and, further, how both theories require dialogue.[3]

Though he will amend, and occasionally attempt to refine, his definition of pragmatism—or *pragmaticism,* as he later preferred—

Peirce never wavered from the central pragmatist insight of the relationship between human purposes and human knowledge, between our "knowing the meaning of a hypothesis and knowing what experiential consequences to expect if the hypothesis is true" (Misak 3). Early in his writings, when Peirce initially formulated this insight, he did so in terms of what he eventually came to refer to as the Pragmatic Maxim: "Consider what effects, that might conceivably have practical bearings, we conceive the object of our conception to have. Then, our conception of these effects, is the whole of our conception of the object" (*Collected* 5: 402). But since we cannot always know in advance, or with absolute certainty, what "effects" or consequences our present conceptions might have in the future, we are met with the unavoidable problem of belief and doubt—a problem that, perhaps more than any other, defined the course of early pragmatist thought, and a problem, which, not surprisingly, Peirce devotes considerable attention to in a number of his essays.

In light of this problem, one of the interesting revisions that Peirce makes in his original definition of pragmatism is the very inclusion of such a "would-be" conditional. Peirce moves from a position of implied certainty, which holds that a specific effect *will* occur, to a more modest view that "a certain kind of sensible effect *would* ensue, according to our experiences hitherto" (*Collected* 5:457; see also 5:453). The difference seems to be a fairly minor one, except that Peirce's latter formulation is, it seems, far more consonant with a pragmatist version of truth—inasmuch as Peirce offers us one for consideration. Which, somewhat reluctantly, he does.

Peirce rejects both "correspondence" and "transcendental" accounts of truth, noting that each assumes an unmediated truth, a truth able to exist somehow apart from human inquiries, purposes, and consequences. Truth, for Peirce, cannot be divorced from the very human condition of belief and doubt; and, when in mock dialogue, Peirce answers questions put to him by the more metaphysically-inclined character of "Mr. Make-Believe," Peirce tells his questioner that "your problems would be greatly simplified, if, instead of saying that you want to know the 'Truth,' you were simply to say that you want to attain a state of belief unassailable by doubt." In the same passage,

Peirce offers his interlocutor still another possible definition: "[I]f you were to define the 'truth' as that to a belief in which belief would tend if it were to tend indefinitely toward absolute fixity, well and good" (*Collected* 5:416).

For Peirce, just as signs without interpretants would not be possible, neither would truths without beliefs. For a pragmatist, these terms are inseparable. Even if we were to attain that sublime condition of belief "unassailable by doubt," we still "cannot in any way reach perfect certitude or exactitude" or infallibility (*Collected* 1:147). But here we run into the sort of perplexities that typically beset readers of Peirce. Why, for example, should we not consider a belief that is "unassailable by doubt" to be a "perfect certitude"? And why would any belief need to "tend *indefinitely* toward absolute fixity" (my emphasis) if attaining such a state would, by definition, settle the question at hand once and for all? To understand why Peirce seems confusing on this point, we must first understand what he is trying to accomplish in his formulation of pragmatic truth.

Peirce wants to keep some version of realist truth that is more certain than subjective opinion but less certain than absolute infallibility. To negotiate such a position, Peirce must discover a pragmatist brand of objectivity, one that embraces belief and doubt as constants that inevitably attend all human inquiry:

> [T]he objectivity of truth really consists in the fact that, in the end, every sincere inquirer will be led to embrace it—and if he be not sincere, the irresistible effect of inquiry in the light of experience will be to make him so. This doctrine seems to me ... to be a corollary of pragmatism. ... I call my form of it "conditional idealism." That is to say, I hold that truth's independence of individual opinions is due (so far as there is any "truth") to its being the predestined result to which sufficient inquiry *would* ultimately lead. (*Collected* 5:494)

Peirce adds that, as a practical matter, "questions do generally get settled in time" and that that is enough (*Collected* 5:494). What's important for Peirce is that truth must have pragmatic value. This value resides not solely in the effects that would follow from a particular truth if embraced; it refers, as well, to our common efforts to attain those truths. Therefore, one important pragmatic value that truth has is that it serves as a *regulative ideal* to which all our inquiries are directed. Truth leads, shapes, guides, prompts, and, in large part, determines our inquiries. And while, in a very limited sense, truth may transcend "experience and inquiry here and now," as Cheryl Misak points out, "it does not transcend experience and inquiry altogether" (41). In her comments on Peirce's conception of pragmatic truth, Misak reminds us again of the conditional quality of his formulation: "A true hypothesis, or a permanently settled belief," for Peirce, "is simply one that *would be*, at the hypothetical end of inquiry, settled" (42).

It follows, then, that because truth cannot be separated from inquiry, neither can it be separated from dialogue. We have seen in chapter one how Bakhtin makes this very point. In composition studies, though, the one scholar who has understood this most clearly and consistently is Peirce's foremost explicator, Ann E. Berthoff. In many of her essays, Berthoff has repeatedly argued that a triadic theory of meaning, a theory that proceeds on the basic assumption that we must interpret our interpretations, is one thoroughly saturated in the processes of social dialogue, in what she refers to, borrowing from I. A. Richards, as "the continuing audit of meaning" ("Rhetoric" 284). Realizing that dialogue is *required* by Peirce's theory of meaning, Berthoff will come at dialogue from various angles, sometimes claiming dialogue to be cognate with dialectic as entailed by the continuing audit of meaning (Meaning 45). On other occasions, though, she will reveal a more pointed concerned with dialogue *per se*. For example, drawing upon the often vexing relationship between interpreter and interpretant, Berthoff alludes to Peirce's (somewhat uneasy) suggestion that "man is a sign." If this is so, she observes, and if it is true, as Peirce claims, that "each sign requires another for its interpretation, it follows that each person requires others in order to understand and be understood: dialogic action requires dialogic partners." The audit of meaning, Berthoff reminds us, "is *necessarily* carried out in societal contexts. . . . Nobody makes meaning by himself or herself" ("Rhetoric" 285).

Not surprisingly, then, Peirce always thinks of meaning—and the pragmatic truths to which meanings tend—as a *movement forward* within social or communal contexts. Perhaps this idea is nowhere better expressed than when Peirce discusses the nature of that special category of signs called thought:

> Finally, as what anything really is, is what it may finally come to be known to be in the ideal state of complete information, so that reality depends on the ultimate decision of the community; so thought is what it is, only by virtue of its addressing a future thought which is in its value as thought identical with it, though more developed. In this way, the existence of thought now depends on what is to be hereafter so that it has only a potential existence, dependent on the future thought of the community. (*Collected* 5:316)

Thought (and we may include here the family of terms to which it belongs—meaning, interpretation, belief) is always addressed to future thought. The process by which "one sign gives birth to another, and especially one thought brings forth another," Peirce calls *pure rhetoric,* a definition that ties rhetoric to the unceasing enterprise of meaning-making, and one that therefore lends considerable force to Berthoff's efforts to recover rhetoric as fundamentally a hermeneutic art (*Collected* 2:229). In any event, what remains obvious is that, for Peirce, interpretation requires dialogue and dialogue requires a future. Or, in the succinct words of one of Peirce's commentators: "It takes time to mean something" (Mounce 26).

A TEMPORARY CONCLUSION

It is interesting to note that drawing upon Peirce's semiotics, Berthoff objects to structuralist-inspired theories because they emphasize a *dyadic* rather than a *triadic* approach to the problem of meaning. In one familiar version of structuralist method, the reader seeks to identify those binary oppositions within a "text" that reveal the system of meaning, or "code," which in turn authorizes all signi- fications to be found within that text. A method like this one, Berthoff claims, fosters "killer dichotomies," the most illuminating of which is *fact* and *opinion,* a dichotomy that implies that real "facts" somehow exist apart from someone to interpret them. For Berthoff and for Peirce, a semiotics of unmediated meaning, a dyadic semiotics, is one that has effectively shut down "the dialectic of meaning and knowing" and, in so doing, any necessity for dialogue whatsoever.

Bakhtin likewise, and understandably perhaps, is critical of methods that derive from structuralist approaches, though he himself will not make any such distinction between dyadic and triadic semiotics. In fact, for one whose thought is sometimes characterized in opposition to semiotics of any kind, it is intriguing to consider how Bakhtin might favorably regard the semiotics of Peirce. As I have tried to show above, there are some notable similarities. Both Bakhtin and Peirce reject the possibility of first and last words. True, Peirce will embrace the usefulness of hypothetical last (or "settled") words, but, along with Bakhtin, he too will insist that *"meanings* are inexhaustible" (*Collected* 1:343). Both thinkers, moreover, regard meaning as ineluctably *addressed,* and therefore each understands meaning as a generative process occurring within historical time. Finally, Bakhtin and Peirce, while hardly foundational thinkers, nonetheless aspire to rescue the concept of truth from the relativism of what they regard as subjective opinion and the absolutism of objective certainty. Peirce's self-described "conditional idealism" is an attempt to navigate a passage through these hazardous extremes, and, as I suggested in the first chapter, Bakhtin's superaddressee seems likewise to posit the need for a regulative ideal by which the seeming futilities of the relativism/absolutism binary might be surmounted.

What, then, of Bakhtin's outsidedness? Or more exactly, what can Peirce tell us about how outsidedness might be construed as a dialogic concept?

Peirce, I think, would not deny that there exists a non-interpretive sense of the outside, one premised upon the brute placement of objects in relation to one another. In Peirce's lexicon, this is the quality of "secondness." But once we add a third, that is, once we take into account the interpretive possibilities of an outside position, as Bakhtin insists we do, then we must necessarily find ourselves already *in dialogue.* If, in other words, meaning is always defined by addressivity, as Peirce maintains it is; and if, furthermore, meaning is always characterized by movement forward in social contexts; and lastly, if meaning is therefore always a threshold phenomenon, requiring others and a future, then dialogue, along with the time it requires, is a constituent feature of all interpretation. Thus, where interpretation is present, there can be no outside of pure location.

Not to be too ironic, we are nonetheless obliged to ask: What does this mean? Or, in pragmatist terms, what follows from a Peircean elaboration of the Bakhtinian notion of outsidedness? I think two considerations are suggested by this discussion—one relevant to our classroom practices, the other to our occasional skirmishes with the public at large.

During the last decade, in the wake of Barthes, Althusser, Foucault, and, more recently, Michel de Certeau, a great deal of interest has been extended to spatial metaphors, particularly in the ways that such metaphors help us think of how relations of power effect subjectivities. Thus, in the parlance of our moment, we speak almost casually of "sites" and "intersections," of "politics of location," of "subject positions," of "contact zones," "borders," "margins," and so on. Composition, too, has embraced this metaphor, especially as a way to reveal to our students how their values, their opinions, their identities are shaped by the geographies of class and community, race and family, gender and tradition.[4] The purpose of drawing our students' attention to the several *loci* they inhabit, of course, is to challenge what we often find in our classrooms: the naive belief among many (if not most) of our students that they live their lives as wholly autonomous, undetermined individuals, "free, beyond the contingencies of history and language" (Clifford 39). Of late, one of the ways this problem has been addressed in the writing classroom is that teachers have developed writing assignments that, in some manner or another, ask students to identify the subject positions from which they write. Writing teachers who employ such a practice obviously mean to foster a particular kind of awareness among students, a critical consciousness of the ways that we and our students are determined by larger social and historical forces.

But, again, there are hazards to be found in a too complete embrace of this metaphor. To understand our students' perspectives wholly in terms of spatial placement, of locations and positionings, is to risk looking upon them precisely as we would points on a map—with supreme confidence that, like those points on a map, our students are reliably, inalterably fixed in place.[5] If our students sometimes suffer from a naive belief that their lives are *un*determined, our spatial metaphors, it seems to me, tempt us to look upon those same lives as *over*determined, as lives denied agency, change, possibility.[6] When literally deployed, metaphors of location simply cannot account for time and change, for the *movement forward* required by Peirce's theory of meaning, as well as Bakhtin's understanding of dialogue.

Peirce, in particular, reminds us that an exclusive preoccupation with spatial positioning, that is to say, an understanding of space abstracted from all temporal considerations, guarantees an end to inquiry and the production of meaning. Indeed, for Peirce, the spatial metaphor, "in itself," must remain quite literally *meaningless*—at least to the degree that constructing an absolute dichotomy between space and time is as quixotic as constructing a similar dichotomy between insides and outsides. Such a view, however, might not find favor by a profession that has found the metaphor enormously valuable. Still, our use of the metaphor would be understood by Peirce as abstracted and partial, just as he would likewise regard Bakhtin's use of it in the concept of outsidedness. In both cases, I believe, Peirce would ask us to look not only for continuities rather than dichotomies, but also for the ways a future is presupposed in even the most fastidious uses of this metaphor. Not to do so is to cultivate an illusion that we, our students, and the world we inhabit together exist merely in fixed relation to one another. For, once we proceed to evaluate and interpret our respective positions, once we begin to imagine other positions that we might ourselves occupy, once we discuss our positions with each other, we are, from Peirce's vantage, already situated in both time and dialogue. A purely spatial world (a world, by the way, that can only be posited) is one that is finished, one with no alterable future—and, I trust, hardly one we would want to promote in our classrooms.

Returning to my earlier discussion of composition's often less-than-friendly outsiders, I believe a second observation to be made of Peirce's extension of Bakhtin has to do with the problem of addressivity. Earlier I observed that outside views of composition are ones not typically addressed to those within composition. I noted, in fact, that outside perspectives on composition are largely intended for the "public sphere," a domain composed (for our critics, at least) of even more outsiders to the discipline or the profession at large. The central problem, as I saw it, was how could "outsidedness" possibly be considered dialogic when the many outside perspectives routinely encountered are seldom addressed to us and are therefore ones that expect no answer from us?

Peirce helps us with this problem, I think, by his basic insistence that there is no meaning that is neither addressed nor uninterpreted. Peirce will allow that there are signs that *seem* to be uttered by (or addressed to) no one. On the first of these, Peirce argues that in cases where an apparent utterer cannot be distinguished, what he calls a *quasesitum,* "a sort of substitute for the utterer . . . fulfills nearly the same function" (*Essential* 404). Thus, Peirce argues that, "If a sign has no interpreter, its interpretant is a 'would-be,' i.e., is what it would determine in the interpreter if he were present" (*Essential* 409). In both cases, a "stand-in" is called upon to fulfill a function that Peirce regards as indispensable to his triadic theory of meaning; and in the latter, Peirce returns to his subjunctive conditional for the proxy that he regards as necessary.[7]

A correlate of Peirce's view, I believe, is the intriguing notion that we may *choose* to be an interpretant, or addressee, even for those utterances not obviously directed to us. In our usual understanding, we regard the addressee as something of a passive recipient, someone determined or invoked by the speaker alone. Peirce, it seems to me, asks us to consider whether or not we might *appropriate* for ourselves, and thus for *our* purposes, the addressee function, particularly, but not exclusively, when no seeming addressee is present or even when a certain utterance might be intended for a different addressee. In other words, Peirce invites us to see the addressee as a figure who claims a prerogative to respond to any utterance of his or her choosing. Claiming this prerogative, of course, does not exempt the addressee from the typical problems that attend any dialogic exchange (i.e., how much authority or influence our responses carry with other addressees; the rhetorical appropriateness of our answers; our command of the speech genre in which the provoking utterance was spoken; and so on). But Peirce's addressee, it seems, does exercise a great deal more range than that addressee who, in a very real sense, does not exist until directly spoken to.

And why is that important? In the context of my earlier discussion, Peirce allows us to see why we need not remain silent spectators when others speak *of* us but not necessarily *to* us. In other words, because public representations of composition have both real and potential effects for composition, they are, in a Peircean sense, *meaningful* to us and are therefore worthy of our response. In the spirit of Peirce, then, I would like to recommend that we proceed from the following maxim whenever we encounter outside perspectives on composition: *any public representation of composition is an utterance addressed to composition*. Of course, as with all utterances, we may choose to respond to how we are publicly represented—or, like Victor Vitanza or Sor Juana, we may choose, instead, to exercise a strategic, rhetorical silence. In any case, the point is that we reserve for ourselves the privilege of interrupting dialogues that concern us but are not meant to include us. Just as the presumed value of an outside perspective for us resides in its ability to interrupt our disciplinary conversations in fruitful ways, we must likewise be able to intrude upon the varied public conversations about us. Another way to put this is that any fully realized theory of dialogue must be able to account for voiced interruptions—*critical interruptions*—without which we have only a diminished say in public representations of composition studies. To guarantee our ability to interrupt critically, then, we must be able to choose for whom we will fulfill the role of addressee.

True, there is "much to learn . . . much to appreciate" from composition's outsiders—and "more to be wary of," as Peter Mortensen has recently observed (83).

Mortensen's choice of public critics, much like my own, attests to the fact that there is indeed a good deal of public discourse about composition that we need to be wary of. But do we have the wherewithal to assume the burden of public engagements? In light of our prior struggles to establish legitimacy in the academy, "going public" would seem to require a measure of will and resources that we may not readily have at our disposal. As Mortensen notes, having fought hard to "build credibility within the academy[,] . . . at the end of the day, little intellectual energy remains for the serious task of going public with what we do, with what we know" (182).

But, of course, we must. We must listen and learn from even our most vehement detractors. We must answer those who may speak of us but not to us. We must make ourselves known to a public who otherwise may never encounter an alternate or contested representation of "what we do" and "what we know." In short, we must provoke authentic exchange with our critics and the publics they address. Or, in Bakhtinian terms, we must become proximate outsiders to those who might prefer instead that we remain so far outside the public forum that we will not be heard at all.

But is this enough? Or, to use the parlance of the logicians, is our entry into the public forum *both* a necessary and sufficient condition for altering that sphere? Michael Bérubé, a noted scholar who publishes frequently in public venues, does not think so. Drawing a distinction between "publicness" and "mere publicity," Bérubé maintains that our experiments in "going public" cannot be limited to our wish to be published in the *Village Voice* or *Harper's*. Elaborating this distinction, Bérubé argues that

> Publicness involves a commitment to the idea of the public. Publicity involves putting a few more talking heads on television and cranking up the academic celebrity apparatus. Publicity means nothing if it isn't tied to the idea of publicness, of public ownership and public welfare. The figure of the so-called public intellectual is worthy of attention, then, only insofar as it can be a force in whatever way, and in whatever media, for fostering and popularizing a revivified notion of public good. (*Res* 170)

Of course, we do not need either Bakhtin or Peirce (or, for that matter, Bérubé) to sanction our forays into what is for most of us unfamiliar territory. But we may find them valuable when we reflect upon the larger meanings of our choice to enter the public fray and upon what we might reasonably expect for doing so. If, as I noted earlier, it "takes time to mean something," it also takes time to *change* something, to imagine a different world from the one we inhabit now.

In my final chapter, I will try to show why this is a concern voiced not only by certain academics and intellectuals, but also by the students we teach, however unwittingly they might do so.

6 DIALOGUE AND CRITIQUE
Bakhtin and the Cultural Studies Writing Classroom

> I repeated the line, "the idea was so simple, anyone could
> [have] thought of it, but it was so obvious that it never
> occurred to me." I said that this was what a cultural critic
> needed to be able to do: to notice those simple-seeming,
> obvious things that usually go unnoticed. I said that this
> was what cultural theory was good for, helping us to see
> what is ordinarily invisible to the people who are actually
> members of the culture being studied. I said I thought this
> writer had understood that concept, and had become a
> cultural critic.
>
> *Kathleen Dixon*

In the excerpt above, Kathleen Dixon repeats what she obviously feels to be a crucial line from one of her student's papers, a line that expresses the kind of epiphany that would be pleasing to any writing teacher, but perhaps especially gratifying to those writing teachers who employ a cultural studies perspective in their classrooms. This is so because *insight* for the cultural studies teacher is not simply a fortuitous, cursory moment in the process of rhetorical invention but is, indeed, the very heart of cultural critique.

I would like to suggest, further, that what Dixon reveals in this passage may well be *the* central dilemma faced by instructors who teach from a cultural studies perspective—namely, the difficulty in making a liberatory agenda comport with a distinctive, seemingly privileged way of knowing. Thus, in the epigraph above, Dixon establishes that cultural criticism is incontestably democratic by virtue of its free availability to all ("anyone could [have] thought of it") and yet is, at the same time, necessary because its epiphanies are often "invisible to the members of the culture being studied." The need for the cultural critic, then, appears to rest on the presumed blindness (or inattention) of ordinary people, who, we are led to believe, need considerable help in seeing not merely what the critic sees, but what the critic *sees through*. Further, there exists an underlying suggestion here that the cultural critic is as likely to be at ease in meritocratic realms as in democratic ones. The last line of this excerpt, for instance, recognizes an important accomplishment by the student, followed by the conferral of well-earned praise from the teacher, who bestows said praise apparently on the presumption that the student has some manifest desire to "become a cultural critic" (112).

According to Michael Bérubé, cultural studies discovers itself to be a "volatile enterprise" because the so-called "ordinary people" it seeks to enlighten already have in place "their own descriptive languages for themselves . . . which serve the purposes of enunciating group identities, practices and self-definitions" (*Public* 166). Far too often, the self-definitions held by "ordinary people" are not the ones preferred by cultural critics, who aim to discover "new knowledges for and about ordinary people" (*Public* 176). Cultural studies, a frankly "oppositional" discourse, often finds itself being opposed by the selfsame groups with which it hopes to establish alliances. Notwithstanding its liberatory aspirations, cultural studies is thus seen by many as elitist or authoritarian in its methods and goals.

Of course, that observation has been made before and in several different contexts. Yet the issue is of particular moment to composition specialists because the site of our most important work—as scholars *and* teachers—is the classroom. For this reason, I believe, we are especially attuned to the difficulties involved in knowing how to teach in a manner that respects our students' views and, at the same time, questions the complacencies that too often inform those views. Thus, for writing teachers who adopt a cultural studies perspective, caveats like this one from Donald Lazere speak of the need to establish a degree of balance in the composition classroom:

> I am firmly opposed . . . to instructors imposing socialist (or feminist, or Third World, or gay) ideology on students as the one true faith—just as much as I am opposed to the present, generally unquestioned (and even

unconscious) imposition of capitalist, white male, heterosexual ideology
that pervades American education and every other aspect of our culture.
(195)

Something of a dual sensibility toward students emerges here: a pois-
ing of the actual *and* the possible, a simultaneous nod to experience
and discernment.

Along these same lines, Joseph Harris wonders if doing cultural
studies must necessarily mean "speaking in the name of someone
who fails to see what we do, or who falls for things we don't" (28).
Harris observes that there exists "a deep anti-democratic impulse"
among those who would speak for "the other reader." What results
from this distrust of the other's experience is the (ironically Platonic)
view that *any unwitting other*—reader, student, consumer—basically
"can't be trusted" and should, therefore, be protected "against the
influences of popular and thus suspect texts" (30). Much like Lazere,
Harris senses the need for some balance in our approach to ideology
in the writing classroom. Our classrooms, Harris argues, ought to be
places where students "can write as people who are, at once, both fans
and intellectuals . . . [where] they can write the pleasures as well as the
problems they find in popular texts" (35). Affirming our students'
capacity to simultaneously experience and critique the culture they
live in, Harris maintains, should provide a useful check against the
temptation to make our students into those "other readers" whom we
"speak for" rather than "listen to and learn from" (36).

But what, precisely, are we apt to find out by listening to our students? One likely discovery, according to Bérubé, is that the public at
large (including our students, of course) is *already* accomplished in
cultural criticism, is *already* familiar with many of the operative
assumptions of cultural theory. "Do we," Bérubé asks, "have to introduce publishers, futures traders, and real estate agents [and I would
add, students] to the idea that there's no such thing as 'intrinsic'
merit, that merit is a social phenomenon?" Or likewise, regarding
those who watch *The Larry Sanders Show*, Bérubé asks, "do we really
need to acquaint them with the idea of the simulacrum?" (*Public*
166). The alleged elitism of cultural studies, then, may repose in our

seeming indifference to what ordinary people already know. As Jan Zita Grover puts it, *"that so much* academic cultural criticism . . . proceeds in willed ignorance of non-academics' ability to use and critique the materials of what academics like to believe is their own—and exclusive—toolbox has nurtured an understandable resentment among its putative subjects" (229).

And yet, behind this affirmation of student awareness lurks a rather disconcerting possibility: if our students are already accomplished in cultural criticism, what is it that we presume to teach? Or, more worrisome for writing teachers perhaps, if our students are already able to generate the kinds of insights noted by Dixon and Bérubé and can do so without our help, do we not risk slipping into a kind of *de facto* current-traditionalism wherein our pedagogies are once again confined to "what's left over," that is, to matters of correctness and style? Two answers are typically offered on behalf of teachers at this juncture. One argues that while it is true our students know a great deal about the meanings of popular culture in their lives, they have yet to realize that they possess this knowledge. And since *they don't know they know,* a good measure of teacherly intervention is necessary. Apart from the obviously patronizing attitude embedded in this view ("I know what you know better than you do"), such an answer does little to remove us from the original charge of elitism and, in fact, lends considerable force to arguments that would seek to maintain a hierarchically-ordered classroom.

The second response, a more pragmatic one, revises the first to read something like this: our students know a great deal about the meanings of popular culture in their lives, but they have yet to realize how this knowedge might alter the world they live in. In this praxis-inspired approach, the teacher's responsibility is to help students know how and where they might transform their own history. But as Lawrence Grossberg has observed, such a position assumes "that the teacher understands the right techniques to enable emancipatory and transformative action" (92). I would add that this position also bestows upon the teacher a knowledge regarding which actions are appropriate to which situations, when those actions are to be performed, how and by whom, and perhaps even such tactical minutiae as when to delay action for long-range purposes. In any event, the teacher once again possesses a special knowledge which, as Grossberg points out, "understands history, and people's positions within it, better than they do" (92).

Is there any way, then, to imagine a teacher's role that doesn't require a caste knowledge that teachers and critics possess, but that many students feel intentionally excluded from? I believe this is an urgent question for composition teachers, and one that, as I will argue below, may find an answer in how successful we are in bringing together the distinct, but mutually tempering, virtues of dialogue and critique. Before elaborating this argument, I wish to begin with an example from one of my classes.

AN ILLUSTRATION

Two years ago, I taught a section of advanced composition to a class of students composed largely of English and English education majors. Since this was an "advanced" course, most of my students were juniors and seniors. In addition, most were women, most were white, and most, as they cheerfully informed me, were taking this course because it was required by their particular specialty. As I have done in the past, I selected the most recent edition (then, the third) of Bartholomae and Petrosky's *Ways of Reading* to be the required text for this course.[1] The unit I report on here, "Popular Culture," included two selections by Mark Crispin Miller, "Getting Dirty" and "Cosby Knows Best," and one by John Fiske, "Madonna." This unit created a forum for the student voices to be heard momentarily.

At the beginning of the unit, I hoped my students would engage the brand of popular criticism offered by Miller and Fiske. I assumed that by reading these two critics, by reflecting upon and discussing the kinds of operations that Miller and Fiske were deft at performing—in other words, that by having the right opportunity—my students could "do" cultural critique. The exploratory writing assignment for this last unit, then, was for students to choose a local, cultural phenomenon for comment and analysis. The papers I got in response to this prompt were, however, disappointing. Though I received a predictable smattering of good essays, on the whole the papers had that telltale "flatness" about them, that lackluster quality that makes writing teachers question the assignment that encouraged such responses. What baffled me most was the extent to which my students' papers were at odds with the typically raucous, sometimes heated, always unpredictable class discussions on the assigned readings. For the most part, very little of the energy that animated those class discussions could be heard in my students' essays.

In thinking about this situation, I began to suspect that what truly interested my students had little to do with *The Cosby Show* but a great deal to do with Miller, little to do with Madonna but a great deal to do with Fiske. What genuinely seemed to interest my students was the problem of trying to figure out exactly what Miller and Fiske were up to. Why, my students wondered, are these "reviews" so unlike the reviews we read in newspapers? Who gave critics the "right" to pass judgments on those who watch TV or follow Madonna? Why did they waste their interpretive talents on the banalities of media icons? Why did they see the "ordinary viewer" with such obvious contempt? Who could they possibly be writing this stuff *for?*

Wanting to tap the vitality of our discussions, I devised a final assignment slightly modified from one suggested in our textbook (175):

> Mark Crispin Miller and John Fiske both write extensively about the larger, cultural meanings of what's usually referred to as "popular culture." While they write about different cultural forms or objects, they both try to imagine the mind and response of the consuming public. That is, both Miller and Fiske have a need to theorize the viewer, reader, or listener.
>
> In an essay of three to four (typed, processed) pages, describe and examine the figure of the *consumer* (the "common" viewer or reader?) and the figure of the *critic* (the "uncommon" reader or viewer?) as represented by these two writers. Conclude your essay with your thoughts on the relationship of critics and criticism to the world of the ordinary consumer.[2]

What follows are excerpts from student responses to this assignment, along with my commentary.[3] I begin with a sampling of passages that document my students' resistance to the critiques of Miller and Fiske:

Though Miller and Fiske represent the consumer as the couch potato, I get the feeling that the critics are a bunch of people (and for some reason I always picture men—I guess the women are out buying Shield and pseudo-feminism) smoking pipes and laughing appreciatively at the picture of the consumer. . . . I get the feeling that these articles were talked over in the country club and then put into print so that the critics' friends could see. The critics are obviously not part of the consumer group—they see the "truth" behind the commercials, TV shows, and musicians and don't buy into it. . . . Basically, the consumers are the comedy show for the critics. Whatever will those couch potatoes buy next?

Barbara

Both see the consumer as mindless and naive. Each seems to see himself, the insightful critic, as just the person to show the blind and stupid consumer the way to the light of social awareness. . . . The critic is there to enlighten . . . while the consumer is there to learn how society works through the careful guidance of the critic.

Elaine

Even in our class there was dissension about the Cosby essay because a lot of people in our age group grew up watching Cosby, as well as listening to Madonna and watching commercials. No one likes to be made to look like a fool, especially for doing something that almost everyone does, almost everyday. . . . Maybe the "common world" rejects their essays because members of that world are a part of the subject being looked at.

Sam

But another problem these critics have . . . is their lack of ability to communicate with the "common reader." They write on levels that can only satisfy one another and never break the barrier between themselves, the "uncommon reader," and the "common reader." Because of this fact, they will always get people asking questions like, "What the hell are they writing about anyway?"

Shannon

Either the consumer really is blind to reality and the critic realizes this, or the consumer is not and the critic must construct situations where the consumer is made to *believe* he is blind. At any rate, the critic must

always be, or at least seem, one step higher in perception and knowledge than the consumer. In many ways the cultural critic is no different
from the artistic or literary critic: he depends on the *ignorance* of his
audience.[4]

Alex

Viewers enjoy the [Cosby] show even more because it gives us a way to
pretend that everything is all right in the world. We are attracted to shows
like the Cosby Show because they give us a form of escape. With the
Huxstables we can pretend, if only for thirty minutes, that the United
States does not have an economic problem among minority groups. We
can pretend that our children, of all ethnic groups, are in the same class
bracket and are "getting along."

Carol

Fiske differs from Miller in the sense that Fiske tends to give the consumer
a little more credit. His analysis of Madonna as an icon of popular culture
tries to explore the minds of her fans. . . . Fiske sees the young girls that
emulate Madonna as newly liberated females. His perspective that young
girls use Madonna's cultural imagery to rebel against patriarchy may indicate his willingness to personify those fans as a reflection of his own intel-
lect. At the same time, he tends to acknowledge that the fans may not be
cognizant of someone like Fiske.

Scott

On the surface of things, responses such as these—for the cultural
studies writing teacher anyway—could be read as distressing.
Indeed, my students' comments seem to lend force to the usual
reports of the conservative, if not reactionary, views that our students hold. Yet, while my students clearly resented what they perceived to be "elitist" representations of themselves at the hands of
Miller and Fiske, their responses were, in fact, far more complex than
this sprinkling of excerpts suggests. If my students' writing lends credence to anything, I would argue, it is to the idea forwarded by
Bérubé, Grover, and others that they already possess a "toolbox" able
to equip them with all the necessary implements to perform cultural
critique. More pointedly, I would argue, my students' comments
speak to a need to consider how dialogue might complement the

project of ideological critique, which cultural studies embraces and, indeed, depends upon.

In the pages to follow, I want to demonstrate a Bakhtinian approach to the problem outlined above. I offer this approach knowing that when dialogue is linked to cultural studies, it typically emerges through the pedagogical theories of Paulo Freire, a thinker quite distinct from Bakhtin but one who shares a number of theoretical affinities with Bakhtin's understanding of dialogue. Such affinities, for example, can be seen in Diana George's and Diana Shoos's attempt to illustrate Freire's eschewal of "sectarian" impositions (left or right) to address the problem I have tried to formulate here:

> If we judge our students' work by whether or not they come to the same conclusions we do, we not only send them conflicting messages about their own worth as thinkers but also insure our own failure as teachers. The function of teachers within the paradigm of a liberatory pedagogy is to allow and encourage our students to become radical thinkers in the sense of coming to their own conclusions, given a raised consciousness. (201-02)

George and Shoos argue that the best way to accomplish such a goal is to establish dialogic classrooms "of exchange and reciprocity" (206). They recommend, among other things, choosing texts about which the teacher has not formed any final judgments so that students and teachers can engage the kind of dialogic inquiry that Freire sees as transformative.

But whereas choosing texts unfamiliar to both teacher and student, no doubt, helps to establish the conditions for mutual inquiry, an exclusive focus on content does not guarantee a dialogic pedagogy. It may well be that at some moment in the process of exploring a "new" text, for example, the teacher's insights become the tacit standard, the official line to which students feel considerable pressure to conform. As teachers, moreover, do we really wish to exclude from our classrooms all those texts that we already have some familiarity with, that we've thought over, struggled with, maybe even changed our minds about? Clearly, then, we need to turn our attentions to the manner in which we present texts, to the ways we might conceive pedagogies that foster the kind of dialogic exchange that Freire, and others, wish to effect. Mikhail Bakhtin, I believe, can help us in this project—though perhaps not in the manner we have typically come to expect.

PROBLEMS OF BAKHTINIAN CRITIQUE

It is by now something of a commonplace that Bakhtin's value to critique may be limited, if not altogether suspect. Certainly, there are any number of appropriations that enlist Bakhtin in service to critical projects, but these appropriations tend to put aside that substantial body of work that falls under the rubric of what Michael Bernard-Donals calls the "phenomenological" Bakhtin, a thinker whose concerns are largely ethical and aesthetic and whose thought is decidedly shaped by the neo-Kantian milieu that he sought to address. On the other hand, those who find in Bakhtin a thinker who might contribute to any project of cultural critique typically draw on the "social" (or what Bernard-Donals and others call the "Marxist") Bakhtin, relying extensively on certain works of the 1930s and 1940s, or sometimes assigning dual or pseudonymous authorship to Bakhtin of earlier works signed by his colleagues, V. N. Volosinov and Pavel Medvedev. Though the authorship question is too thorny and persistent to adequately broach here, what certain scholars find in these works (especially those signed by Volosinov) is a powerful social semiotics from an avowedly Marxist perspective. And yet, the wellspring for much, if not most, Bakhtinian-inspired critique is to be found not so much in the disputed texts, but rather in those works of the 1930s and 1940s. And the single most important concept to be appropriated from these writings is the idea of *carnival,* a theme found in a number of essays but most thoroughly elaborated by Bakhtin in *Rabelais and His World.*

Carnival, though, has proven to be a highly vexed and problematic notion. To be sure, carnival is the chosen turnstile through which many Bakhtinian ideas gain entrance into the arena of cultural studies. And for good reason. Not only does carnival place an enormous faith in popular forms of resistance, in the ability of the "lowly" to travesty the high monologism of all things official, authoritative, and sacrosanct, it does so without patronizing or dismissing the folk and their potential for insurgent laughter. In this respect, Bakhtin seems to have avoided the cultural elitism of, say, Frankfurt-school Marxism, which, as Michael Gardiner has pointed out, "vastly underestimated the heterogeneity and variety of contemporary culture, and how these cultural forms absorbed and reflected many different elements and influences in ways that simply could not be reduced to standardization and political or ideological domination" (189). Gardiner mentions Theodore Adorno's famously contemptuous remarks on jazz as perhaps the most obvious example of how Eurocentric ideological criticism has a long tradition of looking at popular culture as "irrevocably degraded or commodified" (189).

That said, Bakhtinian carnival has been vulnerable to the charge that it represents a lamentable naiveté regarding the workings—subtle, disguised, or overt—of the forces of power and domination. More damning, perhaps, is the view that carnival is not so much a reversal of existing social hierarchies as it is a sanctioning of their legitimacy—a criticism that looks upon organized, "permitted" laughter as complicitous in the power arrangements it parodies or travesties. Subversive laughter, in other words, may not be all that subversive when at carnival's end, the temporarily-suspended hierarchies of a dominant order return with a ferocity that is happily assented to by all. In such an event, it would appear that carnival's primary function is to insure that the authentically transformative moment is missed or forgotten, that emancipatory possibility is siphoned off by a thoroughly orchestrated laughter, which, when all is said and done, amounts to little more than a celebration of what it purports to mock. Such, at least, is a rough sketch of what I understand to be the putative failings of Bakhtin's carnival (see, for example, Bernstein; Gardiner 178-82; Eagleton, *Benjamin* 148).

While I do not underestimate the difficulties in making Bakhtin's ideas "square" with present forms of cultural critique and while I, too, would agree that carnival is a notion that has serious limitations in this regard, I think that if we look more closely at his entire corpus, we might find other possibilities, other entry points for a Bakhtinian understanding of how cultural critique might appear in our classrooms.

ANACRISIS AND THE SUPERADDRESSEE

I want to offer two Bakhtinian concepts, *anacrisis* and the *superaddressee*, for the purpose of bringing dialogue and critique more closely together. Bakhtin's discussion of the former is best addressed in an early work, *Problems of Dostoevsky's Poetics;* and his discussion of the latter is best explained in one of his last essays, "The Problem of the Text," from *Speech Genres and Other Late Essays.* Of the many ideas to be found in Bakhtin's rich corpus, these are perhaps two of the more unlikely concepts to fulfill my announced purpose. That is, anacrisis and the superaddressee would typically be thought to represent Bakhtin at his most traditional and humanistic—anacrisis because it seems to affirm a Platonic understanding of dialogue and the superaddressee because such an idea seems to champion a transcendental worldview. But let us examine each a bit more closely.

Anacrisis

In his study of Dostoevsky, Bakhtin identifies two "basic devices" of the Socratic dialogue: *syncrisis,* which Bakhtin defines as "the juxtaposition of various points of view," and *anacrisis,* which he defines as "the provocation of the word by the word" (110-11). These definitions are offered within the context of Bakhtin's efforts to ascribe to Socrates a dialogic approach to truth and "human thinking about truth" (110). But in order to make this ascription, Bakhtin must separate what he understands to be the novelized genre of the Socratic dialogue from the heavy-handed, catechistic, philosophical monologism of Plato. He does so by arguing that Socrates—the Socrates of the early dialogues, at least—rejects the "ready-made truths" of the later dialogues. That is, according to Bakhtin, this early Socrates had yet to be transformed into a "teacher" (in the strictly pedantic sense of that title), and the Socratic dialogue had yet to enter service to the "worldviews of various philosophical schools and religious doctrines" (110).

This early Socrates, Bakhtin argues, knew that "truth" was neither born nor found in individual consciousness, but rather was something that could only occur *"between* people collectively searching for truth, in the process of their dialogic interaction." As an expert questioner, Socrates was, of course, accomplished in the arts of anacrisis: "He knew how to force people to *speak* . . . to drag the going truths out into the light of day." And the most important consequence of these promptings was to dialogize thought, to "turn [thought] into a *rejoinder*," and likewise, we may assume, to turn all extant truths into rejoinders as well—answers to the provocative words of others (111).[5]

But "going truths" is a telling phrase. Not only does it imply that the one truth usually associated with Platonic epistemology is rather the many truths of dialogue, there is also the clear suggestion that these multiple truths are passing ones, that is, truths that are temporally-situated, contingent. Anacrisis, then, like the project of cultural studies, aims to expose the historicity, the conventionality of the truths we embrace. And yet, the task of revealing situated truths is one made peculiarly difficult by the conditions of our moment. Neither the early Socrates, nor the early Bakhtin, for that matter, could have anticipated how the "going truths" of *our* time and place are disseminated through the ubiquitous venues of popular culture. Nor could either thinker have foreseen the sophistication with which our going truths are purveyed, especially the manner in which they are simultaneously disguised and invoked. These limitations notwithstanding, the characteristic feature of anacrisis, according to Bakhtin, is that it *compels* the participatory word; and to the extent that contemporary forms of popular culture may be interrogated by the participatory word, the writing classroom seems to be one obvious site for anacritic explorations. The project of uncovering the hidden truths of the day, therefore, is a *dialogic* one, a task characterized by mutual inquiry ensuing from the provocative words we speak and engage, the utterances we author and answer.

But isn't this too simple an explanation? Doesn't such an appropriation leave a great deal more to account for? As I noted above, Bakhtin's arguments seem to be conveniently indifferent to the power relations that inevitably attend the problem of who may speak to whom and under what conditions. This charge is familiar enough among those who hear in the valorized term, "dialogue," a liberal-humanist palliative. But Aaron Fogel has shown us that it is not only the celebrated term "dialogue" that is susceptible to this charge; "anacrisis," as well, is a word that bears scrutiny.

Fogel notes that Bakhtin's usage of "anacrisis" is one at profound odds with the word's etymology. In its ancient Greek sense, "anacrisis" referred to a form of interrogation often accompanied by torture. Later, in Roman law and in allusions to Roman law in Pauline scripture, "anacrisis" becomes more commonly associated with a sort of preliminary hearing leading to a formal trial. As Fogel is quick to observe, Bakhtin's usage renders the term even more benign, removing from it any hints of physical violence or legal compulsion, so that the term can be properly fitted to Bakhtin's conception of a dialogic truth. Fogel suggests that Bakhtin must possess a remarkable innocence to not be aware that all speech is constrained—and that some speech is violently constrained. Fogel rejects a conception of "'dialogue' as simple interpersonal freedom, as something inherently 'mutual,' 'sympathetic,' or 'good'" (193).

But Fogel makes a number of rhetorical moves that are in direct opposition to Bakhtin's understanding of dialogue. Fogel's suggestion that Bakhtin's usage of anacrisis veers from the original meaning of that word seems to carry with it a certain prohibition against the kinds of revoicing that Bakhtin saw as inevitable and productive. Moreover, this impulse toward an originary can also be seen when Fogel imagines an oedipal scene for dialogue, a locus for social contracts that govern how dialogues within the group—be these "Quaker meeting, the talk show, 'playing the dozens,'" (193) and so on—are to proceed. One effect of these implicit claims about the possibility of first words (a possibility that Bakhtin denies, of course) is to enable Fogel to emphasize the initiatory, if not originary, quality of coerced speech. Fogel points out that "if there is to be 'dialogue,' someone must make it happen"(193), an assumption that leads him to posit an "Oedipus dialogue complex" that fulfills precisely this function (196).

But what if the words of the provocateur are provoked themselves? Missing from Fogel's understanding of anacrisis, in other words, is its *responsive* character. Fogel seems to imagine what Bakhtin does not: a first speaker who is not only capable of disturbing the "eternal silence of the universe," but whose coercive speech is able to return the universe to a desired quiescence. So figured, anacritic speech—whether in the voiced words of the inquisitor, the lawyer, the teacher—is something wholly autonomous, uncomplicated and unconditioned by prior utterances and anticipated rejoinders. It does not recognize the speech of the oppressor to be thoroughly imbricated in, and thus always to some extent determined by, the speech of the oppressed. And since hegemonic language can be revealed by the hidden polemics that it conducts with those voices that interrogate or oppose it (Bialostosky, "Criticism" 221), one task of what might be called an anacritic approach to cultural studies, then, would be to expose such hidden polemics wherever they may be found.

Of course, the kind of utterance most likely to reveal the hidden polemics that hegemonic discourse conducts is the direct question. Yet, Bakhtin warns that questioning of a certain sort—what he refers to as *pedagogical* questioning—can too easily settle into ritual forms of catechism that are hostile to the unpredictability of authentic dialogue. When that happens, what emerges are *ready-made* answers to *ready-made* questions, and what might have once been "a genuine question," one that allows for the possibility of surprise, has now become, in Nancy Welch's phrase, "a prescription masquerading beneath a question mark" (499). When we ask students to parrot the viewpoints of a Miller or a Fiske or to rehearse the truths we embrace, we serve notice that we aren't especially interested in what they have to say. On the other hand, the corrective to this heavy-handed approach does not mean that we merely recognize and accept whatever "they have to say" in a misguided attempt at benevolent neutrality. Dialogue is likewise abandoned when we fail to *answer* the received, catechistic, well-rehearsed truths that students bring to our classrooms. Allowing their "going truths" to stand unanswered is as contrary to genuine dialogue as requiring that they adopt our own.

And what, then, of *our* "going truths" in the classroom? Or to put this differently, what do we do with the social and political commitments we bring to our writing classes?

True, if our utterances are *only* questions, we might be able to disguise our stances in a pose of disinterested inquiry. But, as Bakhtin reminds us, utterances encompass a broad range of speech genres, and it seems unlikely that we could limit ourselves only to the questions we put to our students. It also seems unlikely, amidst the happenstance

discourse and spontaneous utterances that make up our classrooms—
the desultory asides, comments, silences, assertions, quips, sighs, whis-
pers, and so on—that we could ever hide from students our positions
on the matters we choose to investigate with them under the pretense
of an enlightened neutrality. Yet, Bakhtin would ask, why should we?

> In what way would it enrich the event if I merged with the other, and
> instead of *two* there would now only be *one?* And what would I myself
> gain by the other's merging with me? If he did, he would surely see and
> know no more of me, for in that position he can see and know what I
> myself do not see and do not know from my own place, and he can essen-
> tially enrich the event of my own life. . . . When there are two of us, then,
> what is important is . . . not the fact that, besides myself, there is *one more*
> person of essentially the *same* kind (*two* persons) but the fact that the
> other is for me a *different* person. (*AA* 87)

In the context of this discussion, Bakhtin shows us why the desire
to withhold our own commitments from students, even when moti-
vated by an admirable sense of fairness, is ultimately a mistaken one.
For to the extent that we silence our positions, we withhold from students some measure of the salutary *otherness* that could potentially
enrich whatever understanding they have of their positions. And yet,
at the same time, should we insist that our students merely reprise our
truths, perhaps in the catechistic manner described above, then we
deny to them the very otherness that could enrich *our* understanding.
Take away our mutual *outsider* status in relation to one another, and
we remove from our classrooms the conditions for dialogue and thus,
for Bakhtin, the possibility of *meaning* anything to one another at all.

As teachers, especially teachers of cultural approaches to writing,
we might do well to add to our repertoire of pedagogical roles the figure of *provocateur*, one who drags the "going truths out into the light
of day," one accomplished in the dialogic arts of anacrisis. This means,
among other things, that we encourage the responsive word but not
the silencing one, the probing word but not the last one. Any dialogic
understanding, Bakhtin tells us in the Dostoevsky book, can happen
only *between* people "collectively searching for truth, in the process of
their dialogic interaction" (110). Short of this, we risk becoming the

kind of teacher who would flourish in what Bakhtin refers to as "an environment of philosophical monologism." That is, we become "someone who knows and possesses the truth" and who gladly "instructs someone who is ignorant of it and in error" (81). In such an environment, *no one could possibly change anyone else's mind*—surely an unwanted (if not ironic) consequence for those, like James Berlin and Terry Eagleton, who have suggested clear affinities between ancient rhetoric and contemporary forms of ideological critique.[6]

So far, I have given emphasis to a teacher's perspective on dialogue in the cultural studies writing classroom. A student's perspective, however, might be better illuminated by a very different Bakhtinian concept.

The Superaddressee

In *Speech Genres and Other Late Essays,* Bakhtin provides the fullest account of his theory of the utterance. After exploring the qualities that determine his "metalinguistics," Bakhtin introduces us to a sort of hovering figure that he identifies as a "constituent aspect" of every utterance, an invisibly present third party beyond the second party, who is embodied in the person of our immediate addressee. Bakhtin refers to this third party as the superaddressee and under-stands such a third party to be an inevitability of speaking. This is so because speakers require of their words an "absolutely just responsive understanding" and realize that, if present circumstances are unlikely to provide such an understanding, other dialogic contexts must be— and inevitably are—invoked in the very act of utterance.

One of the key functions of a superaddressee is to provide speakers with a "loophole" through which the oppressions of immediacy might be relieved or avoided. In fact, Bakhtin is rather incredulous toward that speaker who apparently has no need whatsoever of a third party, who finds the temporary understanding wrought from those "on hand" to be adequate (*SG 127*). Bakhtin realizes that authoring an utterance, however innocuous such an activity might seem, is always a hazardous undertaking. From the speaker's perspective, uttering is ineluctably fraught with the potential—some might say likelihood—of infinite misunderstandings. Because this is so, we hedge our (speakerly) bets by invoking a third party, who will listen to us, who will understand perfectly what we have to say. We do so realizing that we simply cannot depend upon our immediates for the understanding we desire.

And yet, far more disastrous than not being understood is the possibility of *not being heard at all*. Something inescapably violent accompanies those contexts where no hearing is possible. Hence, for Bakhtin, "there is nothing more terrible than a lack of response," and thus there is no hell as absolute as the hell of not being heard (*SG* 126-27). The very act of uttering, then, demands that we face not only the possibility of being misheard, but also the possibility of *no available hearing whatsoever*. And to avoid this terror, we invoke another listener, a potential respondent who is at once "invisibly present"and (necessarily) elsewhere. Along with Michael Holquist, we might be tempted to ask why else would unrecognized artists continue to create when there is no obvious audience for their work? Why else would people surrender their lives for causes whose ends they themselves will not live to see? Why else do ordinary folk continue "to hope that outside the tyranny of the present there is a possible addressee who will understand them" (*Dialogism* 38)?

Given the examples offered by Holquist, we might surmise that what allows "poets," and "martyrs," and "quite ordinary people" to act at all is the possibility for an understanding beyond the limited one available to us in existing circumstances. The suggestion here is that our ability to act cannot be separated from our ability to posit, to imagine, to hope for future contexts where our words have a just hearing. Another way to put this is that we cannot avoid constructing normative "utterances" by and through our actions. For Bakhtin, the reverse is true as well: because utterances are acts, which is to say, because utterances are intoned with value, they invoke a more perfect hearer—or, rather, a more perfect context for hearing—than the one available to us in our immediate circumstances.[7] In one Bakhtinian sense, then, *to say is to say what ought to be*.

This is why I think Bakhtin's third party is better thought of as a *rhetorical* figure than a transcendental one. Rhetoric, of course, has a long tradition of acknowledging the exigencies of the immediate situation, the contingencies of present circumstances, the discursive complexities of the here and now. Rhetoric, however, does *not* have a tradition of examining contexts beyond the most immediate and obvious or of examining how such remote contexts might also have a determining function on what speakers say and on the sorts of audiences they imagine in their words. From a rhetorical perspective, Bakhtin's laundry list of possible superaddressees (e.g., "God, absolute truth, the court of dispassionate human conscience, the people, the court of history, and so forth" [*SG* 126]) speaks to a common need to forward our utterances to a context where they may receive a just hearing. What seems to intrigue Bakhtin is what he refers to elsewhere as "the problem of distant contexts," those invoked places and moments where the superaddressee *listens from*.[8] Understood this way, Bakhtin seems primarily interested in how "distant contexts" may be discovered within immediate ones— or more precisely, how normative possibilities are always already present in the very act of utterance.

As I pointed out in chapter one, this idea bears a remarkable similarity to Jürgen Habermas's theory of communicative competence, especially his Chomsky-inspired notion of an "ideal speech situation" that may be reconstructed from "systematically distorted" instances of actual speech. Habermas believes all discourse to be warped by extra-discursive forces—so much so, in fact, that the mutilating influences of dominant ideology pervade "from the inside out," as it were, all of our utterances, all conversational exchanges of any kind. But while Habermas believes that ideological distortion is systematic, he does not hold that it is all pervasive. And because he does not regard it to be complete, Habermas is able to claim (à la Chomsky) that our common, everyday words contain within their saying a deep structure of rational communication, a clue as to what a "perfect hearing" or, in Habermas's terms, an "ideal speech situation" might consist of ("Theory" 371). As Terry Eagleton says of Habermas, so long as dialogue is coercively restrained, our utterances of necessity "refer themselves forward to some altered social conditions where they might be 'redeemed'" (*Ideology* 130).

Although there are important differences between the two, the Habermasian "ideal speech situation" sounds very much like the

Bakhtinian superaddressee, especially when we focus on the contextual rather than the personal implications of the latter.[9] In fact, viewed from a Habermasian perspective, the superaddressee is required precisely because inequalities habitually obtain between interlocutors, because dialogue is always constrained by the power interests that impinge upon it. The superaddressee, in other words, may signify Bakhtin's tacit recognition of the very thing he is often charged with ignoring: namely, the asymmetric relationships of power that shape the manner and direction in which any given dialogue is to proceed. When our utterances are constrained, silenced, misunderstood, interrupted, or otherwise unacknowledged, we quite understandably invoke a better context for their hearing than the one in which we speak. And for this reason, the superaddressee may prove to be useful in our approaches to critical pedagogy.

I believe there are (at least) two ways that the superaddressee could be introduced to writing classrooms that incorporate a cultural studies perspective. The first has to do with the classroom analysis of popular forms and representations, such as our critiques of magazine ads, billboards, sitcoms, movies, lyrics, web pages, and so on. To offer one method suggested by Bruce McComiskey, we may choose to turn our attentions to how, say, a given advertisement fits within a cycle of production, distribution, and consumption—emphasizing, in particular, the heuristic value of these moments to our analysis of cultural processes. But the superaddressee concept might serve a similar heuristic function by suggesting that we examine the manner in which that same ad may offer clues to desirable conditions beyond its own "saying," whether it intends to or not. Recalling Fredric Jameson on this point, Terry Eagleton explains how a "utopian kernel" might be discerned within even the most commonplace of materials:

> Ideologies, cultural formations, and works of art may well operate as strategic "containments" of real contradictions; but they also gesture, if only by virtue of their *collective* form, to possibilities beyond this oppressive condition. On this argument, even such "degraded" modes of gratification as pulp fiction encode some frail impulse to a more durable fulfillment, and thus dimly prefigure the shape of the good society. (*Ideology* 183-84)

In other words, with sufficient effort, we may come to discover that our most pervasive and everyday ideological materials point to "some more desirable state of affairs in which men and women would feel less helpless, fearful, and bereft of meaning" (184). To illustrate how this might be so, Eagleton alludes to Walter Benjamin's study of 19th century Parisian society, a context wherein Benjamin "finds a buried promise of happiness and abundance in the very consumerist fantasies of the Parisian bourgeoisie" (185). Perhaps more relevant to this discussion, Eagleton mentions Ernst Bloch, who, in his *Principle of Hope*, was able to discern "glimmerings of utopia" within "that most unpromising of all materials, advertising slogans" (185).

Taken together, what these thinkers suggest is that our critiques must not be limited to exposing contradictions, unmasking cultural codes, revealing the dominant interests that shape contemporary discourse. Our critiques must also seek to discern the possible in the actual, to discover within the imposed limits of our present situation those "hoped for" contexts where people might feel "less helpless, fearful, and bereft of meaning." The latter is no less a project of uncovering and surely no less demanding of our effort and imagination.

In my own class, for example, *The Cosby Show* was vehemently defended by my students against what they felt to be unfair criticisms offered by Mark Crispin Miller. A common theme in my students' responses to Miller centered upon why he chose to "tear down" the good life presupposed in images of the Huxstables as a flourishing, happy, well-educated, upper-middle class black family. Miller's point, of course, is that such images are meant to camouflage the palpable antagonisms that exist between races and classes in late-twentieth-century America. In Miller's view, the "good life" proffered by the Huxstables is little more than a consumerist fantasy land, a showcase for pricey merchandise, exquisitely appointed interiors, and conspicuously fashionable sweaters.

But if we take seriously the idea that even *The Cosby Show* might be able to suggest altered social conditions—"glimmerings" of hope, so to speak—then both Miller and my students need to be challenged: Miller because he appears to be satisfied not to *offer* any alternative to the "good life" presented by *The Cosby Show;* my students because they seemed content not to *imagine* any alternative to the same "good life." Part of my task, then, was to explore with students what *else* the Huxstables might tell us about other possibilities besides the obvious ones available to us in the drama itself. I began by asking students to think about what social realities the show might be trying to address. What conditions, in other words, might these images of affluence be compensation for? If we choose to imagine the show as a symbolic "corrective" to certain social ills, exactly what are those ills, and what is the Huxstable vision of the kind of "good life" where those ills no longer exist? Or, to put the same point in Bakhtinian terms, if we think of the Cosby show as an *answer* to certain oppressive conditions, is it therefore a *satisfactory* answer? Is it the *only* answer? And if together we can imagine an alternative to the good life presupposed by *The Cosby Show,* what would it be like? How would it differ from everyday life with the Huxstables? Where might it be the same? Questioning of this sort reinforces the notion that any critique of social reality must entail a social imaginary as well.

The second way the superaddressee might be useful in our classrooms is far more reflexive. If, as I have argued, the superaddressee represents Bakhtin's unspoken awareness that differences in power and privilege do, indeed, determine who may speak to whom and under what conditions, then the superaddressee invites us to turn our attention to the classroom as the most obvious context where dialogue is largely shaped by the asymmetric relationships that exist between teachers and students. There may be considerable value in exploring, then, the constraints upon dialogue in our classrooms. Which, for example, result from teacher policies? Which from institutional demands? Which from tacitly agreed-upon conventions and expectations? Additionally, how do such constraints dictate the manner of speaking in class, and in what ways do such forces shape the writing done for this particular course? Lastly, of course, can we posit a better context for learning—and learning to write—than the one we currently inhabit together? And if so, what can we do to make that imagined context an actual one?

Those readers familiar with liberatory pedagogy will see that we have returned to that linchpin of Freirean dialogics, *conscientização,* a deepened historical and situational awareness that enables intervention or transformative praxis. Less obvious, perhaps, is the fact that Bakhtin's superaddressee reiterates another key Freirean theme, one that gained increasing importance in Freire's later writings but was evident throughout all of his work. This is the theme of hope.

> Nor yet can dialogue exist without hope. Hope is rooted in men's incompletion, from which they move out in constant search. . . . Hopelessness is a form of silence, of denying the world and fleeing from it. The dehumanization resulting from an unjust order is not a cause for despair, but for hope, leading to the incessant pursuit of the humanity denied by injustice. Hope, however, does not consist in crossing one's arms and waiting. As long as I fight, I am moved by hope . . . . Dialogue cannot be carried on in a climate of hopelessness. If the dialoguers expect nothing to come of their efforts, their encounter will be empty and sterile, bureaucratic and tedious. (80)

Understood in the way I have outlined here, Bakhtin's superaddressee may embody the very hope to which Freire refers—a hope for discursive contexts that allow for a more just hearing, hope of imagined futures where our deepest sense of what a "good life" entails might yet be redeemed.

COMMITMENT FRAUGHT WITH POSSIBILITY

I began this chapter by setting forth a problem that too often, I believe, accompanies a cultural studies approach to writing instruction—namely, the perception among students that cultural critique is a privileged, elitist mode of inquiry, one that is largely indifferent to, if not contemptuous of, those it presumably seeks to enlighten or liberate. I then argued that a dialogic, specifically Bakhtinian approach to response could help us address this problem and offered a discussion of how two Bakhtinian concepts— anacrisis and the superaddressee—might be applied to our writing classrooms.

Underlying what I have attempted here is my belief that cultural critique *needs* dialogue to restrain its tendencies for authoritarian pronouncements, for "last word" truisms and disabling certainties, for what Freire would call its *sectarianism*. But, likewise, dialogue

needs critique to oppose its often blithe indifference to power relations and to how these relations shape the very conditions for speaking and, of course, writing. Composition teachers who see the value
of *both* dialogue and critique will, however, be faced with a difficult
negotiation. Willing neither to silence our own commitments nor to
require that the same be espoused by our students, desiring from
students neither an intimidated assent nor an unchallenged answer,
teachers who embrace both dialogue and cultural studies find themselves inhabiting an always precarious territory of the between. In
our class discussions, in our assignments, in our responses to student
work, as well as in every other aspect of our pedagogies, we pitch
camp on the *borderlines,* for there and only there are we able to meet
our twin obligations to mutual inquiry, to dialogue, and to the critique of how popular forms underwrite existing power relations in
the most quotidian of ways.

If we fail to inhabit this borderline, I believe, our writing courses
will likely engender the sorts of resentments that led one of my students, Sam, to suspect that in the eyes of critics, he is little more than
a fool. Or, for another, Barbara, to cast herself (defiantly) as a "couch
potato," the kind of person she believes to be more deserving of her
loyalties than the cultural critic. Without a stake and a say in how
their experience should be investigated, represented, and understood
by the many others eager to speak for them, our students will make
little sense of cultural studies. And while this state of affairs is sometimes understandable, it is not inevitable.

ENDNOTES

NOTES FOR CHAPTER 1

1. Crewe here is paraphrasing Knapp and Michaels's argument, a posi-
    tion with which he disagrees.

2. After de Man's early observation of the same, this acknowledgment
    might by now seem to be an unnecessary one (*Resistance* 110-11). The
    enlistment of Bakhtin as antitheorist is a more recent development
    and, as I try to show, a more problematic one. No less concerned with
    the epistemological features of Bakhtin's thought, Michael Bernard-
    Donals has offered a somewhat dichotomized version of Bakhtin's
    ideas, one that posits a continual shifting between the Marxist and
    phenomenological poles found in his works (*Between*).

3. Bakhtin appears to be heading toward the same kind of ironic dis-
    tinction that besets pragmatists when speaking of belief and true
    belief. Bakhtin (at least in this work) seems to want to have it both
    ways: an absolute truth subsumed into the unrepeatable event of
    being, yet somehow able to retain a quality of absoluteness. The
    implied distinction, of course, is between a *theoretical* absoluteness
    and an *experiential* absoluteness, the former imposed from without,
    the latter lived from within. The same distinction is at play in his
    later conception of the superaddressee.

4. Two key pragmatist answers to the charge of relativism can be found
    in Rorty (*Consequences* 166-69) and Davidson ("On the Very Idea of
    a Conceptual Scheme"). Thomas Kent, who, like many others, finds
    social constructionism (one version of antifoundationalism) to be
    particularly vulnerable to the relativist charge ("Discourse
    Community"), offers an excellent discussion of Davidson.

5. Bakhtin's distinction between theory and a sense of theory occurs in
    an appendix to *Problems of Dostoevsky's Poetics*. Written in 1961 and
    published posthumously, this appendix is a collection of notes pre-
    sented in varying degrees of elaboration. One of the least developed
    ideas found here, in fact, is Bakhtin's cryptic distinction about theory.

6.   There is an intriguing (though limited) parallel here with Jürgen Habermas's theory of communicative action. For Habermas, the conditions for a just understanding can be found in actual discourse, no matter how ideologically distorted any particular discourse may be. As Terry Eagleton points out, Habermas is thus able to "anchor the desirable in what is actual" to the extent that "the very *act* of enunciation can become a normative judgment." There is, in other words, a necessity for utterances (and the truth claims they imply or express) to "refer themselves forward to some altered social condition where they might be 'redeemed'" (*Ideology* 130-31).

This sounds very much like the function of Bakhtin's superaddressee, except for one crucial difference: Habermas moves from this observation to the search for a regulative model of the "ideal speech situation" (*Theory* 25) for what Thomas Kent refers to as "the *langue* of *parole*" ("Hermeneutics" 284n). Habermas thus seeks to identify what is universal, rule-governed, and repeatable in instances of perfect communication. Bakhtin has no such desire, since to generalize such qualities is to fall prey to the very theoretism that he disavows.

7.   There is much in Bakhtin's idea of the superaddressee that merits further discussion: his intimation that superaddressees are, to some degree, historically constrained; his problematic silence on the question of how people come to *share* a superaddressee and whether or not it is possible to do so architectonically, that is, without yielding to the temptation to cast the superaddressee as a spokesperson for a generalized, monologic truth; and finally, his claim that absolutes can be subsumed as constituent moments of unrepeatable lived experience. In all these aspects, Bakhtin's superaddressee should continue to pose interesting problems and useful challenges to come.

8.   For one mapping of these intersections and departures, see Bialostosky ("Pragmatic" 107-11).

NOTES FOR CHAPTER 2

1.   This point is further emphasized in an interview with Vadim Kozhinov, one of Bakhtin's literary executors. Kozhinov, upon first meeting Bakhtin, was greeted by the Russian thinker's preemptive admonishment: "Do not think I am a literary scholar, I am a philosopher" (Rzhevsky 56).

2.   Permission granted from the author of the student texts used in this essay.

3.   As I point out at the beginning of the next chapter, there are, of course, other frames within which we can understand student resistance to our teaching of Freire. Richard Miller has recently commented on the frustrations he encounters when, in teaching Freire, the usual occurs: students either resist the "politicization" of the classroom, or they parrot ideas they don't comprehend or believe. Miller asks us to understand this phenomenon in terms of James C. Scott's division between "public" and "hidden" transcripts, the former consisting of what the dominant and the dominated say to each other in open contexts; the latter what they say among themselves when "offstage." This dynamic bears a remarkable similarity to the requirements of Aesopian language; and, in fact, Devlyn's responses can be understood as a partial, somewhat guarded "breaking through" of the hidden transcript into a public sphere where it may very well risk assorted reprisals and consequences.

4.   For an excellent discussion of the complexities involved in Bakhtinian understandings of audience, see Halasek (57-82).

NOTES FOR CHAPTER 3

1.   In composition studies, voice has long been the concern of expressivist rhetorics and, for that reason, our received understandings of voice tend to derive from the work of Elbow, Murray, Coles, et al. What's to be avoided in offering any "new" understanding of voice, then, is the temptation to make expressivist rhetorics into a kind of uniform straw man, which is hardly necessary. It is just as easy— and mistaken—to ignore the differences among those who speak for expressivist rhetorics as to ignore the similarities between expressivist understandings of voice and the ones I discuss here. Expressivist rhetorics, for example, have always understood that voice bears a direct relation to the self and that the intonational qualities of language are rhetorically compelling, insofar as they reveal the perspectives, values, and attitudes "behind" the explicit message or argument. The key difference, however, resides in the origins and nature of the self that is expressed. As I understand expressivist rhetorics, the voicing self is social to the extent that it addresses, and is *influenced by* other voices. But the self I argue for

here is *constituted of* those other voices. In his more recent explorations of voice, Elbow seems to move cautiously toward this viewpoint, allowing that "a self is deeply social—an entity made up largely of strands or voices from others and subject to powerful forces outside itself" ("Pleasures," 230). I say "cautiously" because in describing the self as an "entity" that is "subject to" outside forces and is "largely" composed of other voices, Elbow reveals a measure of uneasiness, I believe, in subscribing to a wholly social understanding of selfhood, the kind upon which my argument is based. For a recent explication of dialogic selfhood, see Taylor ("Dialogical").

2.   Discussing Vygotsky in tandem with Bakhtin is by now fairly common. One reason for such a pairing derives from the notion that Bakhtin is considered to have elaborated what is merely implied by Vygotsky's research (see Emerson, "Outer"; Wertsch, "Significance" and *Voices*). It must be acknowledged, though, that Vygotsky is somewhat more reserved in his views regarding the extent to which language is able to account for the totality of experience. His refusal to equate thought with speech (a necessity if one posits a relationship between the two) and his recognition that language is but one of many sign systems (albeit the most important one) able to mediate psychological activity—these mark off certain nonlinguistic aspects of experience unattended to by Bakhtin. And yet, for both Vygotsky and Bakhtin, the word is *"the significant* humanizing event," since as Caryl Emerson points out, "one makes a self through the words one has learned, fashions one's own voice and inner speech by a selective appropriation of the voices of others" ("Outer," 255).

3.   For a closer look at Vygotsky's quarrel with the "metaphysical" or essential self, see his critique of William Stern's "personalist" psychology in the third chapter of *Thought and Language*.

4.   The metaphors implied by these various terms are revealing. Though Vygotsky sticks to *internalization* with regularity, Bakhtin alternately uses *assimilation, appropriation,* and *expropriation*. The latter two terms derive from property relations and lend some force to arguments for a Marxist Bakhtin. Yet Bakhtin is closer to Vygotsky's *internalization,* I believe, when using the term *assimilation,* since both terms imply a conversion process that occurs in early childhood development. Importantly, neither Vygotsky nor

Bakhtin sees the process of internalization (assimilation) as mere duplication, as a simple imprinting of what is already there in outward form. Rather, both see this process as *transformative*—for Vygotsky, functionally transformative; for Bakhtin, ideologically so.

5.   The passage referred to is taken from *The Diary of a Writer*. The scene involves a dialogue among six workmen, each of whom uses the same common obscenity to express a number of contextually laden, but perfectly understood meanings.

6.   James V. Wertsch has used Vygotsky and Bakhtin to explore the importance of voice for researchers in cognition. Wertsch transcribes several dialogues of teacher-child dyads in an attempt to reveal something of the process whereby the latter appropriates speech genres from the former. Wertsch's research is extremely important, not only for the many concrete illustrations it provides, but for extending the idea of semiotic mediation to include voices. See Wertsch, in particular, *Voices*.

NOTES FOR CHAPTER 4

1.   Our count of publications about imitation differs considerably from Connors's. Though we do not know his particular methodology or exactly how he defined imitation, we surmise that our study is generally broader in scope and more inclusive of how imitation has been approached in fields adjacent to composition studies (e.g., English education, speech communication, etc.), but not strictly within our disciplinary boundaries proper. Of course, the inclusion of these related disciplines bears precisely upon his argument: when composition studies emerged out of these other disciplines, according to Connors, sentence rhetorics, such as imitation, experienced their greatest popularity. Our trends, for the most part, confirm his own, and we generally agree with his conclusions. Where we depart, however, is on the question of whether or not imitation must be considered exclusively within the province of the sentence.

2.   In addition to those postmodern thinkers that Minock identifies as possible sources for a revivified understanding of imitation, the work of René Girard has garnered some recent attention as well. In a response to Richard Boyd's "Imitate Me; Don't Imitate Me," Robert Brooke has sought to understand the mutual resistances

that occur between teachers and their students in the context of Girard's work on mimetic desire and its consequent rivalries. Brooke speculates, as well, that Girard may offer us a framework for understanding how both the freshman student and the freshman writing programs they inhabit can be understood as scapegoats for institutional versions of mimetic rivalry. Conversely, Brooke points out that composition teachers often exercise what Girard calls "renunciative identifications" with the victims of the scapegoating process as, say, when we ally with students and Freire against the structure of institutional oppressions. Brooke doesn't explore the pedagogical implications of Girard's work as much as he does the professional, but he does suggest a promising avenue of inquiry along mimetic lines.

3. Yet, the idea that there may be some affinity between these two terms is an old one indeed. In his *Handlist of Rhetorical Terms*, Richard Lanham identifies "dialogismus" as a cross-reference for "mimesis," noting the former to be defined as "speaking in another's character" (52). In some considerable measure, of course, it is precisely the complexities of "speaking in character" (broadly understood) that Bakhtin explores.

4. See especially Sullivan, who identifies three "aspects of the modern temper" that make it difficult, if not impossible, to "appreciate imitation" in the same way our ancestors could (15): "the myth of progress," "the romantic emphasis on genius," and "the technological mindset." The second of these aspects, Sullivan argues, results from the Romantic substitution of "genius for invention" (16). Recent scholarship, however, has challenged this view of Romantic rhetoric and its putative manifestation in expressivist pedagogy. See Roskelly and Ronald; Gradin.

5. This feature of Bakhtinian subjectivity has recently been critiqued by Jeffrey Nealon. Linking the Bakhtinian subject to the "bourgeois, appropriative self" of Horkheimer and Adorno, Nealon contrasts the Bakhtinian subject with the version of subjectivity proposed by Emanuel Levinas. Bakhtin serves as a rather stark foil for Levinas in Nealon's comparison.

6. I admit to being one of those few. See my "A Language of One's Own."

NOTES FOR CHAPTER 5

1. In keeping with the accepted method of citing Peirce, all references are to volumes and sections of his *Collected Papers* (*Collected*), except for occasional references to *The Essential Peirce* (*Essential*), where page numbers are indicated.

2. One recent development on this very point, in fact, emerges from feminist appropriations of Peirce. In particular, Teresa de Lauretis, Susan Jarratt, and, more recently, Kristie Fleckenstein, have all noted the importance of the body in Peircean semiotics.

3. In a remarkable insight, Peirce denies that, for the pragmatist, there's not much difference between "what one *means* to do and the *meaning* of a word." These two senses of the word, Peirce maintains, are quite kindred, in fact. Peirce thus explains that "when a person *means* to do anything he is in some state in consequence of which the brute reactions between things will be moulded [in] to conformity to which the man's mind is itself moulded, while the meaning of a word really lies in the way in which it might . . . tend to mould the conduct of a person into conformity to that to which it is itself moulded" (*Collected* 1:343). It is difficult to paraphrase Peirce, but I understand him to say that when someone means something, that person anticipates a future event to occur in the way that it has been conceived or imagined, particularly in its intended effects. The meaning of a word, on the other hand, is that which, if believed, brings about the "conduct" intended by the one who utters it. Notice, again, how meaning, whether as intention or definition, is both consequential and conditional, always oriented toward future contingencies.

4. A recent and noteworthy discussion of the implications of the spatial metaphor can be found in Nedra Reynolds's "Composition's Imagined Geographies." Reynolds's article illustrates just how practically difficult it is to exclude time from discussions of space. Her stated emphasis on space, interestingly enough, relies a great deal on juxtapositions with time, especially in her use of the Marxist concept of "time-space compression." Reynolds notes, moreover, that composition has long relied on the spatial metaphor, citing, among other sources, Darsie Bowden's examination of the "text as container" metaphor so familiar to teachers of writing. What's

missed, though, is the fact that the dominant metaphor in composition studies has been a *temporal* one, namely, the "writing as
process" movement. Indeed, the process metaphor could very well
be understood as a response to the spatial metaphors that largely
informed current-traditional rhetorics. In like manner, our current
fascination with spatial metaphors could be understood as a challenge to the hegemony of process approaches, if for no other reason
than spatial metaphors allow us to see the social and political implications of writing pedagogy.

5.   It may be objected that I have overlooked the distinction between
place and space, a distinction especially important to Michel de
Certeau. In *The Politics of Everyday Life,* de Certeau argues that the
term "place" is characterized by a certain stability, while the term
"space" refers to something more mutable, changing. In de Certeau's
view, my argument would hinge on a confusion of these terms. I
would argue in response that these terms imply each other: it is not
possible to imagine a place that exists within no space whatsoever;
nor is it possible to imagine a space that does not include a place,
even if that place serves only to mark the boundary of the space in
question. It seems to me that de Certeau wants to guarantee for the
spatial metaphor some way to explain movement and change. Again,
I would argue that this is not possible within the province of space
alone. Such a project can only be accomplished chronotopically.

6.   I use the term, overdetermined, here in a more obvious, far less
technical sense, than formulated by Louis Althusser. For a discussion of Althusser's conception, see Althusser and Balibar.

7.   Peirce's "stand-in" recalls Volosinov's "hero" of discourse. In fact,
both Peirce and Volisinov use situated utterances to illuminate
their respective notions of the ways a common, tacit understanding informs, precedes, and, indeed, makes possible any particular
understanding of a given utterance. Volosinov's "Well!" (99) thus
aligns nicely with Peirce's "Fine day!" (*Essential* 407) as examples of
concrete utterances that surpass any strictly linguistic explanation.

NOTES FOR CHAPTER 6

1.   I would be remiss if I did not acknowledge Alan France's evaluation
of *Ways of Reading,* particularly the third edition, which I used.
France is congenially disposed to this work but finds in its strong

textual emphasis "an acquiescence in the extant distribution of power" that rivals "expressivism's autonomous subject" (602). The authors' (post)structural textualism is set against France's preferred "materialist reading," and while the third edition receives greater praise than the earlier two, it likewise comes up short in its wavering "commitment to a Marxist critique" (606). This rather severe judgment upon the leftist credentials of *Ways of Reading*, interestingly enough, recalls a criticism leveled at cultural studies in general—a criticism, according to Michael Bérubé, inclined to describe cultural studies as "Marxism Lite," hegemony as a "kinder and gentler" domination, and the practice of cultural studies as "a way for neopopulist intellectuals to get down with the people by writing about how much everybody loves *Terminator 2* and *Murphy Brown*" (*Public* 139-40). While not denying that cultural studies departs from received forms of Marxist thought, Bérubé defends cultural studies against these charges, pointing out where it differs significantly from traditional Marxisms in ways that are clearly useful, compelling, and historically appropriate. Though I feel no similar need to defend *Ways of Reading* against France's critique, I would suggest that France lends credence to the strong textualism he decries by apparently suggesting that teachers and students are unable to appropriate this text in ways that the editors did not intend or could not imagine.

2.   Knowing that my students were aware of my sympathies both for cultural studies and for their resistance to it and self-conscious of my obvious affiliation with that caste of "privileged revealers" who inhabit English departments, I specified myself as the audience for this assignment. I did so believing that having to write for *this* (very) familiar audience might complicate their writerly task in ways that could be rhetorically instructive—or failing that, occasionally interesting. What emerged, though, were papers whose collective need to answer Miller and Fiske encouraged my students to write for each other, perhaps as a community under siege, rather than for their originally-stated audience. In fact, this served as the occasion to draw an ironic parallel to a charge I heard often in our class discussions, that critics like Miller and Fiske are capable of writing only for other critics like themselves.

3.   The author would like to express gratitude to all members of his English 3810-001 class, Spring of 1995, especially to those whose

work is cited here. Permission to use excerpts from student authors was obtained prior to the submission of this manuscript. All names are fictional.

4. In one sense, what Alex offers here is a version of what Bernard Williams (after Aristotle) calls the *Coriolanus paradox,* a reference to those who "tend to defeat themselves by making themselves dependent on those to whom they aim to be superior" (39).

5. For a fuller discussion of Bakhtin's appropriation of Socrates, see Zappen.

6. See, for example, Eagleton's *Literary Theory,* especially 205-217. It might be suggested that I have confused a traditional Aristotelian rhetoric of persuasion with the redefinition offered by Eagleton that emphasizes the effects of discourse in social and cultural contexts. But these are hardly unrelated concerns. Any understanding of cultural studies will proceed on the assumption that the question of how minds are made cannot be separated from the problem of how minds are changed.

7. In identifying "attitude" as the "sixth term" of his Pentad, Kenneth Burke may help explain this point. Burke defines attitude as *incipient* action, and since for Bakhtin, the tones of our words reveal, more than anything else, our attitudes, our "slants on the world," then every utterance we make is not simply a "literal" act; it is also the positing of a future act that has yet to come to fruition but that nonetheless motivates what we utter in the immediate contexts in which we speak (Burke 443).

8. In fact, Bakhtin will often allude to this problem in other essays of the period, as well as in comments that he made before his death in 1975. In an interview with Sergei Bocharov, Bakhtin reveals that he "was fascinated by the problem of distant contexts—I started working on it several times back in the 1920s, but I didn't get very far, beyond starting." After which, Bakhtin adds ironically, "There was no distant context for such a work" (Bocharov 1021).

9. The most obvious difference is that Habermas wants to identify a regulative model of the "ideal speech situation." As noted earlier, Habermas thinks it possible to apprehend what is universal, rule-governed, and repeatable in instances of perfect communication, to ascertain what Thomas Kent has called "the *langue* of *parole*" (284n). Unlike Habermas, Bakhtin has no such desire.

WORKS CITED

Althusser, Louis, and Etienne Balibar. *Reading Capital.* Trans. Ben Brewster. London: Verso, 1979.

Altieri, Charles. "Temporality and the Necessity for Dialectic: The Missing Dimension of Contemporary Theory." *New Literary History* 23 (winter 1992): 133-58.

Bakhtin, M. M. *Art and Answerability: Early Philosophical Essays by M. M. Bakhtin.* Trans. Vadim Liapunov. Supp. trans. Kenneth Brostrum. Ed. Michael Holquist and Vadim Liapunov. Austin: Univ. of Texas Press, 1981.

————. *The Dialogic Imagination: Four Essays.* Trans. Caryl Emerson and Michael Holquist. Austin: Univ. of Texas Press, 1981.

————. *Problems of Dostoevsky's Poetics.* Trans. and ed. Caryl Emerson. Theory and History of Literature 8. Minneapolis: Univ. of Minnesota Press, 1984.

————. *Rabelais and His World.* Trans. Helene Iswolsky. Bloomington: Indiana Univ. Press, 1984.

————. *Speech Genres and Other Late Essays.* Trans. Vern W. McGee. Ed. Caryl Emerson and Michael Holquist. University of Texas Press Slavic Series, 8. Austin: Univ. of Texas Press, 1986.

————. *Toward a Philosophy of the Act.* Trans. Vadim Liapunov. Ed. Michael Holquist and Vadim Liapunov. University of Texas Press Slavic Series, 10. Austin: Univ. of Texas Press, 1993.

Bartholomae, David. "Inventing the University." In *When a Writer Can't Write,* ed. Mike Rose, 134-65. New York: Guilford Press, 1985.

————. "What is Composition and (if you know what that is) Why Do We Teach It?" In *Composition in the Twenty-First Century: Crisis and Change,* ed. Lynn Z. Bloom, Donald A. Daiker, and Edward M. White, 11-28. Carbondale: Southern Illinois Univ. Press, 1996.

————, and Anthony Petrosky. *Ways of Reading: An Anthology for Writers.* 3rd. ed. Boston: St. Martin's Press, 1993.

Berlin, James A. "Composition Studies and Cultural Studies: Collapsing Boundaries." In *Into the Field: Sites of Composition Studies,* ed. Anne Ruggles Gere, 99-116. New York: MLA, 1993.

Bernard-Donals, Michael. *Mikhail Bakhtin: Between Phenomenology and Marxism.* New York: Cambridge Univ. Press, 1994.

———, and Richard R. Glejzer, eds. *Rhetoric in an Antifoundational World: Language, Culture, and Pedagogy.* New Haven: Yale Univ. Press, 1998.

Bernstein, Michael André. "When the Carnival Turns Bitter: Preliminary Reflections Upon the Abject Hero." In *Bakhtin: Essays and Dialogues on His Work,* ed. Gary Saul Morson, 99-121. Chicago: Univ. of Chicago Press, 1986.

Berthoff, Ann E. *The Making of Meaning: Metaphors, Models, and Maxims for Writing Teachers.* Montclair, New Jersey: Boynton/Cook, 1981.

———. "Killer Dichotomies: Reading In/Reading Out." In *Farther Along: Transforming Dichotomies in Composition,* ed. Kate Ronald and Hephzibah Roskelly, 12-24. Portsmouth: Boynton/Cook, 1990.

———. "Rhetoric as Hermeneutic." In *College Composition and Communication* 42 (October 1991): 279-87.

Bérubé, Michael. *Public Access: Literary Theory and American Cultural Politics.* London: Verso, 1994.

———. "Res Publica." *Minnesota Review* 50-51 (1998): 165-70.

Bialostosky, Don H. "Booth's Rhetoric, Bakhtin's Dialogics, and the Future of Novel Criticism." *Novel: A Forum on Fiction* 18 (spring 1985): 209-16.

———. "Dialogic Criticism." In *Contemporary Literary Theory,* ed. G. Douglas Atkins and Laura Morrow, 214-28. Amherst: Univ. of Massachusetts Press, 1989.

———. "Dialogic, Pragmatic, and Hermeneutic Conversation: Bakhtin, Rorty, and Gadamer." *Critical Studies* 1 (1989): 107-19.

———. "Liberal Education, Writing, and the Dialogic Self." In *Contending with Words: Composition and Rhetoric in a Postmodern Age,* ed. Patricia Harkin and John Schilb, 11-22. New York: MLA, 1991.

Bizzell, Patricia. "Beyond Antifoundationalism to Rhetorical Authority: Problems Defining Cultural Literacy." *College English* 52 (1990): 661-75.

Bocharov, Sergei. "Conversations with Bakhtin." Trans. Stephen Blackwell. Ed. Vadim Liapunov. *PMLA* 109 (1994): 1009-24.

Bokser, Julie A. "Sor Juana's Rhetoric of Silence." Retrieved 15 November 2000. <http://icarus.cc.uic.edu/~jboksel/silence.html>.

Bowden, Darsie. "The Limits of Containment: Text-as-Container in Composition Studies." *College Composition And Communication* 44 (1993): 364-79.

Boyd, Richard. "Imitate Me; Don't Imitate Me: Mimeticism in David Bartholomae's 'Inventing the University.'" *JAC* 11 (1991): 335-45.

Brodkey, Linda, and James Henry. "Voice Lessons in a Poststructural Key: Notes on Response and Revision." In *A Rhetoric of Doing: Essays in Honor of James Kinneavy,* ed. Stephen P. Witte, Neil Nakadate, and Roger Cherry, 144-60. Carbondale: Southern Illinois Univ. Press, 1992.

Brooke, Robert. "René Girard and the Dynamics of Imitation. Scapegoating, and Renunciative Identification: A Response to Richard Boyd." *JAC* 20 (2000): 167-76.

Burke, Kenneth. *A Grammar of Motives.* Berkeley: Univ. of California Press, 1969.

Caesar, Terry. *Conspiring with Forms: Life in Academic Texts.* Athens: Georgia Univ. Press, 1992.

Certeau, Michel de. *The Politics of Everyday Life.* Trans. Steven Rendell. Berkeley: Univ. of California Press, 1984.

Clark, Katerina, and Michael Holquist. *Mikhail Bakhtin.* Cambridge: Harvard Univ. Press, 1984.

Clifford, John. "The Subject in Discourse." In *Contending with Words: Composition and Rhetoric in a Postmodern Age,* ed. Patricia Harkin and John Schilb, 38-51. New York: MLA, 1991.

Connors, Robert. "The Erasure of the Sentence." *College Composition and Communication* 52 (September 2000): 96-128.

Corbett, Edward P. J. "The Theory and Practice of Imitation in Classical Rhetoric." *College Composition And Communication* 22 (1971): 243-50.

Couture, Barbara. *Toward a Phenomenological Rhetoric: Writing, Profession, and Altruism.* Carbondale: Southern Illinois Univ. Press, 1998.

Crewe, Jonathan. "Toward Uncritical Practice." In *Against Theory: Literary Studies and the New Pragmatism,* ed. W. J. T. Mitchell, 53-64. Chicago: Univ. of Chicago Press, 1985.

Cruz, Sor Juana Inés de la. *The Answer/La Respuesta.* Ed. and trans. Electa Arenal and Amanda Powell. New York: The Feminist Press of The City University of New York, 1994.

Damasio, Antonio. "Review of Research on Prosopagnosia." In *Fields of Writing: Readings Across the Disciplines,* ed. Nancy Comley, et al. 2nd. ed., 525-33. New York: St. Martin's Press, 1987.

Dasenbrock, Reed Way. "We've Done It to Ourselves: The Critique of Truth and the Attack on Theory." In *PC Wars: Politics and Theory in the Academy,* ed. Jeffrey Williams, 172-183. New York: Routledge, 1995.

Davidson, Donald. *Inquiries Into Truth and Interpretation.* Oxford: Clarendon Press, 1986.

Davis, D. Diane. "Review of *Rhetoric in an Antifoundational World: Language, Culture, and Pedagogy,*" ed. Michael Bernard-Donals and Richard R. Glejzer. *Rhetoric Review* 17 (spring 1998): 179-84.

Dixon, Kathleen. "Making and Taking Apart 'Culture' in the (Writing) Classroom." In *Left Margins: Cultural Studies and Composition Pedagogy,* ed. Karen Fitts and Alan W. France, 99-114. New York: State Univ. of New York Press, 1995.

Eagleton, Terry. *Ideology: An Introduction.* London: Verso, 1991.

———. *Literary Theory.* Minneapolis: Univ. of Minnesota Press, 1983.

———. *Walter Benjamin: Or Towards A Revolutionary Criticism?* London: Verso, 1981.

Elbow, Peter. "Closing My Eyes As I Speak: A Plea for Ignoring Audience." *College English* 49 (1987): 50-69.

———. *Landmark Essays on Voice and Writing.* Mahwah, NJ: Erlbaum, 1994.

———. "The Pleasures of Voice in the Literary Essay." In *Literary Nonfiction: Theory, Criticism, Pedagogy,* ed. Chris Anderson, 211-34. Carbondale: Southern Illinois Univ. Press, 1989.

Emerson, Caryl. *The First Hundred Years of Mikhail Bakhtin.* Princeton: Princeton Univ. Press, 1997.

———. "The Outer Word and Inner Speech: Bakhtin, Vygotsky, and the Internalization of Language." *Critical Inquiry* 10 (1983): 245-64.

Farmer, Frank. "'A Language of One's Own': A Stylistic Pedagogy for the Dialogic Classroom." *Freshman English News* 19 (fall 1990): 16-22.

———. "Foundational Thuggery and a Rhetoric of Subsumption." In *Rhetoric in an Antifoundational World,* ed. Michael Bernard-Donals and Richard R. Glejzer. 195-223, New Haven: Yale Univ. Press, 1998.

————, and Phillip K. Arrington. "Apologies and Accommodations: Imitation and the Writing Process." *Rhetoric Society Quarterly* 23 (winter 1993): 12-34.

Fish, Stanley. *Doing What Comes Naturally: Change, Rhetoric, and the Practice of Theory in Literary and Legal Studies.* Durham: Duke Univ. Press, 1989.

Fleckenstein, Kristie. "Writing Bodies: Somatic Mind in Composition Studies." *College English* 61 (January 1999): 281-306.

Fogel, Aaron. "Coerced Speech and the Oedipus Dialogue Complex." In *Rethinking Bakhtin: Extensions and Challenges,* ed. Gary Saul Morson and Caryl Emerson, 173-96. Evanston: Northwestern Univ.Press, 1989.

France, Alan W. "Assigning Places: The Function of Introductory Composition as a Cultural Discourse." *College English* 55 (1993): 593-609.

Freire, Paulo. *Pedagogy of the Oppressed.* Trans. Myra Bergman Ramos. New York: Continuum, 1970.

Gallie, W. B. *Peirce and Pragmatism.* New York: Dover, 1966.

Gardiner, Michael. *The Dialogics of Critique: M. M. Bakhtin and the Theory of Ideology.* New York: Routledge, 1992.

George, Diana, and Diana Shoos. "Issues of Subjectivity and Resistance: Cultural Studies in the Composition Classroom." In *Cultural Studies in the English Classroom,* ed. James A. Berlin and Michael J. Vivion, 200-10. Portsmouth, NH: Boynton/Cook, 1992.

Glenn, Cheryl. *Rhetoric Retold: Regendering the Tradition from Antiquity Through the Renaissance.* Carbondale: Southern Illinois Univ. Press, 1997.

Gradin, Sherrie. *Romancing Rhetorics: Social Expressivist Perspectives on the Teaching of Writing.* Portsmouth, NH: Boynton/Cook-Heinemann. 1995.

Greenhalgh, Anne M. "Voices in Response: A Postmodern Reading of Teacher Response." *College Composition and Communication* 43 (1992): 401-10.

Grossberg, Lawrence. "Pedagogy in the Present: Politics, Postmodernity, and the Present." In *Popular Culture, Schooling, and Everyday Life,* ed. Henry Giroux and Roger Simon, 91-115. New York: Bergin and Garvey, 1989.

Grover, Jan Zita. "AIDS, Keywords, and Cultural Work." In *Cultural Studies*, ed. Lawrence Grossberg, Cary Nelson, and Paula Treichler, 227-39. New York: Routledge, 1992.

Habermas, Jürgen. "Toward a Theory of Communicative Competence." *Inquiry* 13 (1970): 360-375.

———.*Communication and the Evolution of Society*. Trans. Thomas McCarthy. Boston: Beacon Press, 1979.

———. *The Theory of Communicative Action*. 2 vols. Trans. Thomas McCarthy. Boston: Beacon Press, 1984.

Halasek, Kay. *A Pedagogy of Possibility: Bakhtinian Perspectives on Composition Studies*. Carbondale: Southern Illinois Univ. Press, 1999.

Harris, Joseph. "The Other Reader." *JAC* 12 (1992): 27-37.

Haynes-Burton, Cynthia. "Interview with Victor J. Vitanza." *Composition Studies* 21 (spring 1993): 49-61.

Holquist, Michael. *Dialogism: Bakhtin and His World*. New York: Routledge, 1990.

———. Introduction to *Speech Genres and Other Late Essays*, by M. M. Bakhtin. Austin: Univ. of Texas Press, 1986.

Jarratt, Susan. "In Excess: Radical Extensions of Neopragmatism." In *Rhetoric, Sophistry, Pragmatism*, ed. Steven Mailloux. Cambridge: Cambridge Univ. Press, 1995.

Kent, Thomas. "Hermeneutics and Genre: Bakhtin and the Problem of Communicative Interaction." In *The Interpretive Turn*, ed. Davis Hiley et al., 282-303. Ithaca: Cornell Univ. Press, 1991.

———. "On the Very Idea of a Discourse Community." *College Composition and Communication* 42 (1991): 425-45.

Klancher, Jon. "Bakhtin's Rhetoric." In *Reclaiming Pedagogy: The Rhetoric of the Classroom*, eds. Patricia Donahue and Ellen Quandahl, 83-96. Carbondale: Southern Illinois Univ. Press, 1989.

Knapp, Steven and Walter Benn Michaels. "Against Theory." In *Against Theory: Literary Studies and the New Pragmatism*, ed. W. J. T. Mitchel, 11-30. Chicago: Univ. of Chicago Press, 1985.

Kozulin, Alex. *Vygotsky's Psychology: A Biography of Ideas*. Cambridge: Harvard Univ. Press, 1990.

Lanham, Richard A. *A Handlist of Rhetorical Terms*. 2nd ed. Berkeley: Univ. of California Press, 1991.

Lauretis, Teresa de. *Alice Doesn't: Feminism, Semiotics, Cinema.* Bloomington: Indiana Univ. Press, 1984.

Lazere, Donald. "Teaching the Political Conflicts: A Rhetorical Schema." *College Composition And Communications* 43 (May 1992): 194-213.

Lodge, David. *After Bakhtin: Essays on Fiction and Criticism.* London: Routledge, 1990.

Man, Paul de. *The Resistance to Theory.* Minneapolis: Univ. of Minnesota Press, 1986.

McComiskey, Bruce. "Social-Process Rhetorical Inquiry: Cultural Studies Methodologies for Critical Writing about Advertisements." *JAC* 17 (1997): 381-400.

Miller, Richard E. "The Arts of Complicity: Pragmatism and the Culture of Schooling." *College English* 61 (1998): 10-28.

Minock, Mary. "Toward a Postmodern Pedagogy of Imitation." *JAC* 15 (1995): 489-509.

Misak, Cheryl. *Truth and the End of Inquiry.* New York: Oxford Univ. Press, 1991.

Morson, Gary Saul. "Parody, History, and Metaparody." In *Rethinking Bakhtin: Extensions and Challenges,* ed. Gary Saul Morson and Caryl Emerson, 63-86. Evanston, IL.: Northwestern Univ. Press, 1989.

Morson, Gary Saul, and Caryl Emerson. *Mikhail Bakhtin: Creation of a Prosaics.* Stanford: Stanford Univ. Press, 1990.

———. eds. *Rethinking Bakhtin: Extensions and Challenges.* Evanston: Northwestern Univ. Press, 1989.

Mortensen, Peter. "Going Public." *College Composition And Communications* 50 (December 1998): 182-205.

Mounce, H. O. *The Two Pragmatisms: From Peirce to Rorty.* New York: Routledge, 1987.

Nealon, Jeffrey T. "The Ethics of Dialogue: Bakhtin and Levinas." *College English* 59 (February 1997): 129-48.

Peirce, Charles Sanders. *Collected Papers of Charles Sanders Peirce.* Vol. 1-6. ed. Charles Hartshorne and Paul Weiss. Vol. 7-8, ed. Arthur Burks. Cambridge: Harvard Univ. Press, 1931-1935; 1958.

———. *The Essential Peirce: Selected Philosophical Writings.* 2 vols. The Peirce Project. Bloomington: Indiana Univ. Press, 1998.

Putnam, Hilary. *Realism and Reason: Philosophical Papers.* Vol. 3. Cambridge: Cambridge Univ. Press, 1983.

Reynolds, Nedra. "Composition's Imagined Geographies: The Politics of Space in the Frontier, City, and Cyberspace." *College Composition And Communications* 50 (September 1998): 12-35.

Ritchie, Joy. "Beginning Writers: Diverse Voices and Individual Identity." *College Composition and Communication* 40 (1989): 152-74.

Rorty, Richard. *Consequences of Pragmatism: Essays 1972-1980.* Minneapolis: Univ. of Minnesota Press, 1982.

———. *Philosophy and the Mirror of Nature.* Princeton: Princeton Univ. Press, 1979.

Roskelly, Hephzibah, and Kate Ronald. *Reason to Believe: Romanticism, Pragmatism, and the Teaching of Writing.* Albany: SUNY Press, 1998.

Rosmarin, Adena. "On the Theory of 'Against Theory.'" In *Against Theory: Literary Studies and the New Pragmatism,* ed. W. J. T. Mitchell, 80-88. Chicago: Univ. of Chicago Press, 1985.

Ruenzel, David. "The Write Way to Success: 'Feel Good' Writing Deprives Students of Needed Skills." *San Francisco Chronicle,* 5 February 1999, A23.

Rzhevsky, Nicholas. "Kozhinov on Bakhtin." In *Critical Essays on Mikhail Bakhtin,* ed. Caryl Emerson, 52-66. New York: G. K. Hall, 1999.

Sacks, Oliver. *The Man Who Mistook His Wife For a Hat and Other Clinical Tales.* New York: Harper & Row, 1987.

Schuster, Charles. "Mikhail Bakhtin as Rhetorical Theorist." *College English* 47 (1985): 594-607).

Scott, James C. *Domination and the Arts of Resistance: Hidden Transcripts.* New Haven: Yale Univ. Press, 1990.

Smit, David. "Hall of Mirrors: Antifoundationalist Theory and the Teaching of Writing." *JAC* 15.1 (1995): 35-52.

Sullivan, Dale L. "Attitudes Toward Imitation: Classical Culture and Modern Temper." *Rhetoric Review* 8 (fall 1998): 5-21.

Taylor, Charles. "The Dialogical Self." In *The Interpretive Turn: Philosophy, Science, Culture,* ed. David R. Hiley, et al., 304-14. Ithaca: Cornell Univ. Press, 1991.

———. "Rorty in the Epistemological Tradition." In *Reading Rorty,* ed. Alan Malachowski, 257-75. Oxford: Basil Blackwell, 1990.

Trimbur, Joseph. "Beyond Cognition: The Voices in Inner Speech." *Rhetoric Review* 5 (1987): 211-21.

Vitanza, Victor. "Re: Victor Vitanza in Harper's." 13 January 1994. Online posting. H-Net History of Rhetoric Discussion List (H-Rhetor). <hrhetor@uicvm. bitnet>. 15 February 1999.

Volosinov, V. N. "Discourse in Life and Discourse in Art." In *Freudianism: A Critical Sketch*, trans. I. R. Titunik, ed. I. R. Titunik and Neil R. Bruss, 93-116. Bloomington: Indiana Univ. Press, 1987.

Vygotsky, Lev S. *Mind in Society: The Development of Higher Psychological Processes.* ed. Michael Cole, Vera John-Steiner, Sylvia Scribner, and Ellen Souberman. Cambridge: Harvard Univ. Press, 1978.

———. *Thought and Language.* Rev. ed., Trans., and ed. Alex Kozulin. Cambridge: MIT Press, 1986.

Welch, Nancy. "One Student's Many Voices: Reading, Writing, and Responding with Bakhtin." *JAC* 13 (fall 1993): 493-502.

Wells, Susan. "Rogue Cops and Health Care: What Do We Want from Public Writing?" *College Composition and Communication* 47 (October 1996): 325-41.

Wertsch, James V. "The Significance of Dialogue in Vygotsky's Account of Social, Egocentric, and Inner Speech." *Contemporary Educational Psychology* 5 (1980): 150-52.

———. *Voices of the Mind: A Sociocultural Approach to Mediated Action.* Cambridge: Harvard Univ. Press, 1991.

Williams, Bernard. *Ethics and the Limits of Philosophy.* Cambridge: Harvard Univ. Press, 1985.

Yancey, Kathleen Blake, ed. *Voices on Voice: Perspectives, Definitions, Inquiry.* Urbana: NCTE, 1995.

Zappen, James P. "Bakhtin's Socrates." *Rhetoric Review* 15 (1996): 66-83.

INDEX

ABOUT THE AUTHOR

Frank Farmer is an associate professor of English at the University of Kansas, where he teaches courses in writing and rhetorical theory. He received his undergraduate degree from Indiana University, and two graduate degrees from the University of Louisville. Over the course of his career, he has taught in several public schools and universities, including East Carolina University, where he helped to establish a graduate program in rhetoric and composition. His work has appeared in *College Composition and Communication, Rhetoric Review, Rhetoric Society Quarterly, Symploké,* and *The International Journal of Qualitative Studies in Education.* He is also editor of *Landmark Essays on Bakhtin, Rhetoric, and Writing.* He lives with his wife, Linda, in Lawrence, Kansas.